Praise for *When You Can't Pray*

What Christian has not felt that their pleading prayers, apparently unanswered, seem like undeliverable letters? Al Truesdale confronts this reality head on with proper reference to Scripture and a realistic view of life. It's a solid book that never loses sight of the hope that will not disappoint.

The Very Reverend Frank F. Limehouse III
Former Dean, Cathedral Church of the Advent
Birmingham, AL

WHEN YOU CAN'T PRAY

WHEN YOU CAN'T PRAY

FINDING HOPE WHEN YOU'RE NOT EXPERIENCING GOD

Second Edition

AL TRUESDALE

BEACON HILL PRESS
OF KANSAS CITY

Copyright © 2016 by Al Truesdale
Beacon Hill Press of Kansas City
PO Box 419527
Kansas City, MO 64141
beaconhillbooks.com

978-0-8341-3572-7

All rights reserved. No part of this publication may be reproduced, stored in a retrieval system, or transmitted in any form or by any means—for example, electronic, photocopy, recording—without the prior written permission of the publisher. The only exception is brief quotations in printed reviews.

Cover designer: Jeff Gifford
Interior designer: Sharon Page

Library of Congress Cataloging-in-Publication Data

Names: Truesdale, Albert,1941- author.
Title: When you can't pray : finding hope when you're not experiencing God / Al Truesdale.
Description: second [edition]. | Kansas City : Beacon Hill Press of Kansas City, 2016. | Includes bibliographical references and index.
Identifiers: LCCN 2016004364 | ISBN 9780834135727 (pbk. : alk. paper)
Subjects: LCSH: Prayer—Christianity.
Classification: LCC BV215 .T78 2016 | DDC 248.3/2—dc23
LC record available at http://lccn.loc.gov/2016004364

All Scripture quotations, unless indicated, are taken from The *Holy Bible: New International Version*® (NIV®). Copyright © 1973, 1978, 1984, 2011 by Biblica, Inc.™ Used by permission of Zondervan. All rights reserved worldwide. www.zondervan.com.

Scripture quotations marked (NRSV) are from the New Revised Standard Version Bible, copyright © 1989 the Division of Christian Education of the National Council of the Churches of Christ in the United States of America. Used by permission. All rights reserved.

Scripture quotations marked (RSV) are from the Revised Standard Version of the Bible, copyright © 1946, 1952, and 1971 the Division of Christian Education of the National Council of the Churches of Christ in the United States of America. Used by permission. All rights reserved.

Scripture quotations marked (KJV) are from the King James Version of the Bible.

The internet addresses, email addresses, and phone numbers in this book are accurate at the time of publication. They are provided as a resource. Beacon Hill Press of Kansas City does not endorse them or vouch for their content or permanence.

The various stories and scenarios related throughout this book, without corresponding endnote citations, are fictional case studies used for the purpose of illustrating points and demonstrating examples. Any similarity to real people or events is entirely coincidental.

CONTENTS

Introduction	9
1. When Prayer Loses Its Meaning	11
2. Tragedy and the Christian Life	25
3. The God Who Holds Us	35
4. Texts of Frustration	43
5. In Defense of Faith that Complains	63
6. Intercessory Prayer	73
7. The Mystery of Iniquity	85
8. When gods Fail	95
9. In Defense of Doubt	109
10. When God Hides	115
11. Prayer that Words Cannot Express	123
12. Prayer at the End of Life	129
13. No Substitute Jesus	145
Conclusion	151
Notes	153

INTRODUCTION

THE OLD and New Testaments are richly endowed with prayers of God's people, from Solomon's eloquent prayer at the temple's dedication (1 Kings 8:22–40) to the martyr's plea for vindication in Revelation (6:9–11). The pages of church history yield a cornucopia of prayers that display the majestic diversity of the church's journey with its Lord. Many books have been written to instruct congregations and individual Christians. There are books that instruct in prayer for almost every age and occupation. Books about prayer are written for those contemplating marriage, and for persons experiencing divorce. Some books are meant for women and some for men. One tells how prayer "changed history," another how prayer can "change everything," and another promises prayer can "change your life forever" in only thirty days. To make sure no one is forgotten, one book is titled *Christian Prayer for Dummies*.

For some Christians, prayer is a formidable odyssey rather than an enjoyable journey. The mere mention of prayer dredges up memories of frustrating and failed efforts to pray fruitfully. They may recall personal or family struggles when prayer became a barrier instead of a portal for entering God's presence. For others, rather than being an opportunity for productive communion with the

Lord, prayer involves little more than muttering anguished cries about life gone awry, or calling out questions, doubts, and fears.

Instead of the heavenly courts, some Christians occupy the shadowlands. They feel as though they have been consigned to occupy a religious twilight zone. There are more questions—often deeply disturbing ones—than answers.

This book is for those Christians who can't pray, or for various reasons find it difficult. Each chapter seeks to deal honestly with one or more obstacles to communion with God through prayer. The counsel offered is grounded in the conviction that, in spite of all obstacles to prayer, the "God of all grace" journeys with his children—even though the fog of uncertainty may keep him from being seen or heard. But even in the darkness, God is working to draw his children into "his eternal glory" (1 Peter 5:10). Surely the God who carried a young prophet, who—while in despair over failure—cursed the day he was born, will conduct his children through their deepest valleys (Jer. 20:14).

ONE
WHEN PRAYER LOSES ITS MEANING

Elaine's Story

Elaine is the wife of a seminarian who, as a loan officer in an inner-city bank, is "putting hubby through." Communion with God through prayer that yields an increasing love for others is something for which she longs. Recently, Elaine audited an evening seminary course called Spiritual Formation. Instruction in the regular practice of prayer as one dimension of spiritual growth was part of the course. Elaine would love to bring before the Lord challenges she faces while working with people whose credit and employment records make it difficult to obtain loans. But she is encountering frustration that stems from her childhood.

From her youth, Elaine's Christian parents modeled a belief that God is not to be bothered until big problems come along. They seemed to subscribe to the belief that *God gave us brains, so we should use them to solve our problems. Don't bother God with incidental stuff. Keep the heavenly power hitter out of the game until the game is in question. Read the Bible; respond to God's love and mercy in worship; and work diligently to serve those around you.*

Try as she might, Elaine has found it impossible to overcome that way of understanding prayer. She is simply unable to reconcile the two different Gods.

Carl's Story

A husband of twenty-three years and a Christian since childhood, Carl prayed fervently that his wife, Leatha, would be healed of liver metastasis, also known as secondary liver cancer. She underwent extensive chemotherapy. (Liver metastasis develops when primary cancer from some other part of the body spreads to the liver).

The books Carl read about prayer and the encouragement he received from fellow Christians assured him that if his faith was strong enough, Leatha would be healed. Friends came loaded with Bible verses that seemed to support their confidence. Leatha's death, therefore, plunged Carl into a valley of religious despair and self-doubt. Had he failed to pray hard enough, failed to believe?

Drained of energy and spiritual strength, Carl was unprepared for the attempted explanations he received. Friends were confident his faith had not been strong enough. One friend, seeking to console Carl, explained that the Lord had taken Leatha to strengthen Carl's faith.

No sooner had Carl begun to recover from Leatha's death than his son, Raymond, was diagnosed with acute lymphoblastic leukemia (ALL), a fast-growing cancer of a type of white blood cells called lymphocytes. Cancerous lymphocytes crowd out bone marrow and prevent it from making normal red blood cells, white blood cells, and platelets.

The news about his son shook Carl to his foundations. His well-intended Christian friends, who prayed fervently for Raymond, assured Carl that God was too good to permit Raymond to die. Carl agreed. Some of his friends had "prayed through" and been "assured" that Raymond would soon see the "salvation of the Lord." Raymond's ALL, they assured Carl, would go into remission (something that happens after chemotherapy to more than eight out of ten ALL patients).

On a cold, rainy, February afternoon, two years after Raymond's diagnosis, Carl sat beside Raymond's graveside. A religiously devastated man, Carl's resources were exhausted. Like Job, Carl knew he had not failed God. Yet the language of prayer that seemed so easy for others, and that had promised healing for both Leatha and Raymond, was now bankrupt for Carl.

While Carl's pastor spoke of resurrection faith, Carl slowly burned. While he was expected to show hope, he was seized by gnawing doubt, even contempt, about prayer and faith. Intended as words of hope and solace, talk of the resurrection struck Carl as a mockery of simple, believing people such as himself. With steely resolve, he said to himself, "I neither can nor want to pray or believe."

Many Christians have never experienced questions and testing even remotely similar to what Elaine and Carl endured. Some might say, "Elaine just needs to put her childhood memories out of mind." And, "Carl needs to learn to trust the Lord in all things, repent of his resentment, consult his fellow Christians, and get on with his life."

Elaine and Carl's perplexity is far more tenacious and noble than their critics permit, though. Their struggles should neither be dismissed nor condemned. Answers to their questions lie much deeper than simply attributing their crises to poor thinking and faulty faith. Solutions composed of "try harder" misconstrue the pain and sources of their anguish.

Someone else might say Elaine and Carl just don't understand prayer. This may be true, but for them, the obstructions are real and should be taken seriously. Each of them is trying to live as Christians by maps crafted by well-intended people. Yet, consequently, the maps are leading them away from God, not toward him.

Many Christians find prayer difficult, if not impossible. But this much is certain: Because God is as great and loving as the Bible declares, he can absorb Elaine and Carl's frustrations and doubts. Both of them are kept in God's inexhaustible and everlasting care. Hopefully, the Lord will eventually lead them out of the shadows.

A riveting Old Testament story places Christians who struggle with prayer in the company of a minor prophet whose sharp words to God may leave some of us stunned.

Habakkuk's Story[1]

If Elaine and Carl could visit Jerusalem in the late seventh century BC, they might meet a strange prophet named Habakkuk who would understand and share their frustrations. During Habakkuk's time, death stalks Judah. Habakkuk is a zealot for the pure worship of God. He is deeply devoted to the great revival King Josiah initiates (the Deuteronomic Reformation), as recounted in 2 Kings 22–23 and 2 Chronicles 34.

Josiah comes to the throne with a strong love for God, his law, and the temple (2 Kings 23:25). He wants to restore pure worship of God. The revival is an impressive effort to eliminate all pagan worship in Judah.

Amon was the king who preceded Josiah. Before Amon, Manasseh reigned. He was the villain-king of Judah who gave in to the Assyrians by reopening the pagan shrines outside Jerusalem. Earlier, his father, Hezekiah (c. 715–687 BC), destroyed the pagan shrines and practices in one of the most sweeping covenant reforms in Judah's history. But Manasseh tried to combine worship of Yahweh with worship of Baal. He also introduced pagan practices into the Jerusalem temple. As a final surrender to paganism, Manasseh and the people practiced human sacrifice. Manasseh actually burned his own son as a pagan offering (Jer. 7:31).

In contrast, Josiah removes all signs of Assyrian domination and pagan influence. His first efforts at reform begin in 629 BC, the twelfth year of his reign (2 Chron. 34:3). The revival is well underway when, in the eighteenth year of Josiah's reign, a remarkable discovery is made. While making repairs to the temple and cleansing it of pagan objects, workers discover a manuscript—the book of the Law (or, Torah).

When the manuscript (probably Deut. 12–26) is read to Josiah, he tears his garments in despair. The high priest asks Huldah, a prophetess, to verify the document's authenticity. Her response cuts to the nation's heart: Because Judah has grossly violated the covenant, God will bring evil upon Jerusalem.

Shaken over how extensively Judah has sinned, Josiah calls the people to the temple and reads to them the "book of the covenant (2 Kings 23:1–2) that has been found by the workers. Josiah leads the people through a covenant renewal. They vow to obey the Lord completely (2 Kings 23:3). An unparalleled, nationwide, religious reform follows (2 Kings 23:4–20).

Josiah implements the revival with even greater thoroughness than King Hezekiah (2 Kings 18:1–20:21; 2 Chron. 29:1–31:21), Josiah's great grandfather. Hezekiah was one of the most distinguished and celebrated kings in Judah. Under Josiah's leadership, pagan practices are abolished. Canaanite worship of Baal, worship of the heavenly bodies, and worship of other deities ends. Out of the temple and onto the junk pile go all alien objects. The people stop "sacred prostitution," child sacrifice, and wizard consultation. The grand climax of the revival is renewal and celebration of the Feast of Passover. Not since the time of the Judges has there been such a Passover festival (2 Kings 23:21–23).

Josiah destroys the outlying sanctuaries, hotbeds of paganism. He even extends the revival into the old northern kingdom (Israel). He destroys its temple at Bethel and concentrates worship of Yahweh in the Jerusalem temple.

But the doctrine that supports the revival contains a serious flaw. It oversimplifies God's ways in history and makes divine justice too neat. The people are told that if they only obey the law, all will go well. They will receive success or failure, rewards or punishments, dependent upon how obedient they are to a code of rules. Living through this period, the prophet Jeremiah accuses those who espouse this formula of turning the law into a lie (Jer. 8:8).

During Josiah's reforms, the sprawling Assyrian empire is slipping out of control. After 652 BC, flames of revolt spread to Egypt and Babylon. The death of the Assyrian empire comes in 612 BC when Nineveh, the Assyrian capital, falls to a combined attack by the Babylonians, Medes, and Scythians. The Assyrians make an unsuccessful, last-ditch stand at Haran.

Then comes an astonishing turn of events: Pharaoh Necho of Egypt (610–594 BC) decides to rescue Assyria, Egypt's former enemy. He prefers a weak Assyria to a strong Babylon. So in 609 BC he marches north to salvage the remnants of the Assyrian empire.

Meanwhile, in Jerusalem, Josiah learns of Necho's move and decides to side with Babylon. So he marches his army north to the narrow pass of Megiddo, where he intends to cut off the Egyptians and win Babylon's favor.

But things do not go well. Josiah is defeated and slain at the battle of Megiddo. Now good King Josiah, author of the great revival, friend of God, and not yet forty years old, is dead. The cruel events shatter the bargain-counter calculations behind the popular motives for revival. Disillusionment descends as the Egyptians turn Judah into one of its vassal states (2 Kings 23:29–30). Necho continues his march to the Euphrates, where his army is crushed by the Babylonians.

In Judah, a Babylonian yoke—no lighter or more merciful—replaces the Assyrian yoke, and the great revival collapses. As events prove, and as Jeremiah sees, the revival has not resulted in a circumcision of the heart (Deut. 10:16). It did not survive its shallow roots. Within twenty years, almost all signs of revival have vanished. Mosaic faith has been forgotten. And worship of God once again blends into worship of pagan deities.

Where does Habakkuk fit into this picture? He sees it all, including the spiritual rot from Manasseh's apostasy. He cheers the great reforms that seem to sweep paganism from the land. He rejoices to see the temple restored. But he also listens as the gospel of predictable returns is preached.

Habakkuk painfully absorbs the trauma of Josiah's defeat and death, and watches the great revival collapse. Who could question that the revival was God's will? Now, Habakkuk's hopes are dashed and his faith badly shaken. To make matters worse, the Babylonians are moving in.

In his time of crisis, what does Habakkuk say to God, whom he trusted? Because he is the Lord's prophet, we might expect that he patiently trusts the Lord. Does he leave for us an exemplary model of faith in perilous times? No!

Habakkuk cannot pray, cannot trust, and can no longer hope. Rather, he bitterly airs his disappointments and resentments:

O LORD, how long shall I cry for help,
and you will not listen?
Or cry to you "Violence!"

and you will not save?
Why do you make me see wrongdoing
and look at trouble?
Destruction and violence are before me;
strife and contention arise.
So the law becomes slack
and justice never prevails.
The wicked surround the righteous—
therefore judgment comes forth perverted.
(Hab. 1:2–4, NRSV)

Habakkuk asks God, "If your eyes are too pure to behold evil, and if you can't tolerate wrongdoing, then why do you stand silent while the wicked are swallowing up the righteous?" (Hab. 1:13).

As long as the book of Habakkuk remains in the Bible, people like Elaine and Carl will be included in the scope of God's care. God apparently isn't alarmed by honest questions about himself or the meaning of prayer. Later we will hear how God answers Habakkuk.

Some Reasons for a Crisis in Prayer

Prayer can be problematic for Christians for numerous reasons.

First, some people conclude that prayer is meaningless because of the implications of what they are saying when they pray. If God is as dependent on our coaxing as prayer implies, then God is either too lazy or too ignorant to warrant our worship. Christians are supposed to urge God to help the missionaries or assist the persecuted Christians throughout the world or protect children who are at risk.

Why, some ask, should we need to encourage God to do what God ought to be doing anyway? If God sent missionaries, doesn't he already know their needs? Doesn't he already know that Christians in some world areas are being persecuted? Are not vulnerable children already the object of God's care?

If we must urge God to do what we would readily do if we could, then are we not God's moral superior?

Second, prayer becomes meaningless for some because they lose their bearings amidst conflicting instructions. On one hand, they are supposed to ask God specifically for physical healing. On the other hand, they should pray, "Thy will be done." So which is it? If God already has a will in the matter, why make a request that might conflict with it?

Third, related to the second reason, some people find prayer meaningless because they don't see how people can speak so easily about knowing God's will in advance of an event. Then, when things turn out differently, they say the outcome was still God's will.

Fourth, some find it difficult to pray intelligently because often they can't distinguish between what is good and what is evil, what should or should not be petitioned.

Some years ago, Christians in Texas prayed that God would deliver them from an impending hurricane. At the same time, Oklahoma cotton farmers were praying for enough rain to save their drought-stricken fields. When the hurricane arrived, Texas Christians wondered why God had not spared them, while Oklahoma Christians thanked God for the bountiful water.

Given that some things appear good under some conditions but bad under others, how is a Christian to pray intelligently?

Fifth, some reflective Christians are dumbfounded by how God may be praised for acting in one instance while being defended or excused for not acting in another. Philip Yancey tells of a Sunday evening church service during which the pastor reported that during the previous week a plane carrying nine missionaries had crashed in the Alaskan outback. Everyone onboard died. Then the pastor introduced a member of the church who, that same week, had survived an unrelated plane crash. Upon hearing of the narrow escape, the congregation broke out in praise of God; they were confident God had providentially intervened. The congregation had no hesitance about crediting God with one so-called miracle, but they gave God a pass for not saving nine others. How did these Christians know so much about how God does and does not act?[2]

Sixth, the mystery of gratuitous evil in the world, both great and small, paralyzes the ability of many people to pray. The random and senseless visitation of moral and natural evil upon some, and the random escape from evil by others, leaves some Christians disoriented. How in the world are they supposed to ask for God's intervention?

Seventh, theologian Marjorie Suchocki discusses an obstacle to prayer that disturbs some people but that many might ignore. Given the immensity of the universe and our own infinitesimal place in it, how sensible is it to say that God is concerned about "me, my needs, and my prayers"? Perhaps in earlier times, when people believed the earth was the center of the universe, the question would not have surfaced.

Now, however, we know the earth is only one planet in a small solar system, and that our solar system is just part of a galaxy we call the Milky Way—a whirling pinwheel made of one hundred billion, or more, stars. There are tens of billions of galaxies. So what sense does it make to say that the God who created and runs all of this is concerned about one human who occupies just one speck of space and time?[3]

Eighth, for some people, prayer loses its meaning because it seems that the God whom they hear people addressing is just one tribal deity among others. This God exists to protect the narrow interests of a particular nation, denomination, social class, or political party. He even gets called upon to favor one sports team over another!

For those for whom such appeals make prayer unattractive and even trivial, a tribal deity, no matter how big, is still a limited god, unworthy of worship. Confronting the god who is finally nothing more than a tribal deity is perhaps the most tenacious struggle we twenty-first-century Christians face. Nevertheless, before the true God can reign in us, and before prayer can ever become more than special pleading, tribal deities must die. Short of that, God is reduced to a domestic hearth deity (Gen. 31:17–21), who spends his time performing household duties.

Perhaps no piece of literature amplifies this error more powerfully than Mark Twain's famous piece of prose called *The War Prayer*.[4] It was published in 1923, thirteen years after Twain (whose real name was Samuel Clemens) died. His family asked him not to publish the piece before his death for fear that it would sound sacrilegious. Twain said that in *The War Prayer*, he told the whole truth. He exposed the absurdity of praying to a tribal deity—in this case, a deity asked to take sides in a war. Twain was appalled by the aftermath of the Spanish-American War (1898) and the subsequent Philippine-American War (1899–1902).

The War Prayer begins, "It was a time of great and exalting excitement. The country was up in arms, the war was on, in every breast burned the holy fire of patriotism." In one church the building was full of people, including soldiers, "their young faces alight with martial dreams."

Eventually the time arrives for the pastoral prayer. "None could remember the like of it for passionate pleading and moving and beautiful language." The thrust of the minister's prayer is a plea that an ever merciful and benign Father watch over the noble young soldiers. The supplication is that God would aid, comfort, and encourage the volunteers in their patriotic work. God should bless and shield them in the day of battle and their hour of peril. He should hold them in his mighty hand, make them strong, confident, and invincible. In the ensuing bloody conflict, God should help them crush the foe. He should grant to them and to their flag and country everlasting honor and glory.

"An aged stranger entered and moved with slow and noiseless step up the main aisle, his eyes fixed upon the minister, his long body clothed in a robe that reached to his feet, his head bare, his white hair descending in a frothy cataract to his shoulders." Not conscious of the stranger's presence, the pastor continues to pray, ending with a "fervent appeal, 'Bless our arms, grant us the victory, O Lord our God, Father and Protector of our land and flag!'"

The stranger touches the minister's arm as he finished the prayer and silently indicates that the minister should step aside. He says, "I come from the Throne—bearing a message from Almighty God! ...He has heard the prayer of His servant your shepherd and will grant it if such shall be your desire after I, His messenger, shall have explained to you its...full import. For it is like unto many of the prayers of men, in that it asks for more than he who utters it is aware of."

Here now, the stranger says, is what both the pastor and the congregation have silently, if not aloud, also prayed for:

...O Lord our God, help us to tear their soldiers to bloody shreds with our shells; help us to cover their smiling fields with the pale forms of their patriot dead; help us to drown the thunder of the guns with the shrieks of their wounded, writhing in pain; help us to lay waste their humble homes with a hurricane of fire; help us to wring the hearts of their unoffending widows with unavailing grief; help us to turn them out roofless with little children to wander unfriended the wastes of their desolated land in rags and hunger and thirst, sports of the sun flames of summer and the icy winds of winter, broken in spirit, worn with travail, imploring Thee for the refuge of the grave and denied it—for our sakes who adore Thee, Lord, blast their hopes, blight their lives, protract their bitter pilgrimage, make heavy their steps, water their way with their tears, stain the white snow with the blood of their wounded feet! We ask it, in the spirit of love, of Him Who is the Source of Love, and Who is the ever-faithful refuge and friend of all that are sore beset and seek His aid with humble and contrite hearts. Amen.

Twain concludes *The War Prayer* with these words: "It was believed afterward that the man was a lunatic, because there was no sense in what he said."

Who, in fact, was mad? The devotees of their tribal deity completely missed the message from the throne.

TWO
TRAGEDY AND THE CHRISTIAN LIFE

I Would Prefer Not To

One of the most puzzling stories in American literature is "Bartleby the Scrivener: A Story of Wall Street," by Herman Melville.[1] The main character, Bartleby, copies and proofreads legal documents in the New York Office of the Chancery.[2] The master who hires Bartleby describes him as "pallidly neat, pitiably respectable, incurably forlorn!" The master would be happier if Bartleby were "cheerfully industrious." Instead, Bartleby works "silently, palely, mechanically."

At first Bartleby "seemed to gorge himself" on documents, as if famished for work. Then one day, after only three days of employ, things change sharply. The master wants Bartleby to help examine a document and expects immediate cooperation. To the master's surprise, Bartleby responds, "I would prefer not to." Later, when the Master asks his three employees to examine a batch of documents, Bartleby once again responds, "I would prefer not to."

From that day on, in spite of threats, cajoling, and questions, "I would prefer not to" is all Bartleby ever says. He never explains why he abruptly stopped working. Much of the rest of the story traces the master's efforts either to motivate Bartleby, dismiss him, or get away from him.

Eventually Bartleby becomes a vagrant. The police move him to the Tombs—a combination prison, asylum, and shelter for the poor. Bartleby refuses to eat and finally dies of starvation, curled up in a corner of the yard.

As the story concludes, we know nothing more about why Bartleby suddenly "preferred not to" than we did at the beginning. The answer appears in the story's brief conclusion, which Melville calls a "sequel." Bartleby has, in fact, been immobilized by the depth and magnitude of human tragedy.

Before becoming a scrivener, Bartleby worked at the Dead Letter Office in Washington, DC, where he sorted undeliverable letters and burned them "by the cart-load." The story ends thus:

> Sometimes from out the folded paper the pale clerk takes a ring:—the pale finger it was meant for, perhaps, moulders in the grave; a bank-note sent in swiftest charity:—he whom it would relieve, nor eats nor hungers any more; pardon for those who died despairing; hope for those who died unhoping; good tidings for those who died stifled by unrelieved calamities. On errands of life, these letters speed to death.
>
> Ah Bartleby! Ah humanity!

Confronting an endless parade of human pain and tragedy in the Dead Letter Office finally caught up with and overwhelmed Bartleby. "Gorging" on work as a scrivener, he tries to escape his own appointment with tragedy. He fails. Tragedy, in all its force, catches up with him in the Office of the Chancery. Bartleby faces the futility of endlessly copying legal documents in a world plagued by dead letters.

He, perhaps, asks himself: *What am I to make of a world where, even when people try to do what is good, failure and despair often result?* Bartleby decides that continuing to copy documents as a show of normalcy is an insult to those who suffer tragedy. He knows that for them, life seems more like a dead letter than life on Wall Street. Continue to copy? Bartleby "would prefer not to."

We may say Bartleby's analysis of the human situation is too extreme. However, no one who has wrestled with bruising tragedy will dismiss Bartleby's struggle so easily, or say they find it difficult to understand him. Many have, at least temporarily, reached the point where they "would prefer not to."

Christians and Tragedy

Some Christians seem to believe that faith and tragedy exclude each other. In fact, Christians are no more immune to tragedy than anyone else. No amount of prayer or faith can guarantee against it. Failure to candidly confront this fact only compounds suffering. Pollyanna-type responses that minimize the agony of tragedy people endure are sub-Christian.

The good news is that the Christian faith meets tragedy head on and, without overlooking its injury, moves toward redemption.

People have recognized and wrestled with the reality of tragedy at least since the time of the early Greeks in the fifth century BC. We associate efforts to understand and confront tragedy with Greeks such as Euripides, Sophocles, and Aristotle, the German Johann Wolfgang von Goethe, the Englishmen William Shakespeare, Samuel Johnson, and Thomas Hardy, and the Russian Fyodor Dostoyevsky.

What is tragedy? No uniform definition exists. The Greeks mostly thought of tragedy as an inherent weakness in a hero that would finally bring him down. Defeat would spring from an unforeseen and unavoidable defect. But the Greek way isn't the only way to understand tragedy.

Tragedy can also be a life experience in which things go badly awry for unexpected, even incomprehensible reasons that have nothing to do with flaws in one's character or faith. Tragedy can be an evil that results from a collision of circumstances over which we have little or no control, and for which blame usually should not be assigned. German writer Johann Wolfgang von Goethe (1749–1832) said all tragedy depends on insoluble conflict. It thrives in the womb of contradictions.[3]

Tragedy can result from misjudgment and even ignorance but not necessarily from overt vice or depravity. It might even follow in the wake of people trying to do what they thought was right.

One day in July 2000, Sharon Everett, a 51-year-old wife and mother from Fort Thomas, KY, was returning home from the grocery store. Unknown to Sharon, pool chemicals in the shopping bags behind the driver's seat had leaked into other products she was bringing home. As she turned into her driveway, the interior of her car exploded into flames. By the time firefighters got her out of the car, almost 60 percent of her body was covered with third-degree burns. Her ears, eyelids, lips, nose, and hair were all destroyed.[4]

In many instances tragedy can be overcome, as demonstrated by a wealth of inspiring stories. In other instances it cannot be. A disruptive genetic flaw in a newborn, for instance, might place upon a family taxing, lifelong burdens that can be managed but never eliminated.

Often tragedy is a difficult reality for Christians to reconcile with their trust in God and their aversion to sin. We know how to deal with sin, understood as rebellion against God and his righteous reign. We know its source and motivation, and where to place accountability. We also know that rebellion against God can be terminated through repentance and obedience. But that is not the case with tragedy.

Too often, Christians mistakenly tend to equate *sin* with *evil*. The word *evil* includes sin. But it is a larger, more inclusive term. Evil includes sin *and* tragedy, both of which are traceable to the fall of Adam and Eve. To be sure, both sin and tragedy are the enemies of God's *shalom* (peace); both of them introduce disorder into God's good creation.

But while we associate sin with blameworthiness, accountability, and guilt, we must not do that with tragedy. Otherwise, guilt and perhaps shame will be improperly and harmfully assigned. A false, even immobilizing sense of blameworthiness will prevail where it should not.

Unless a distinction between sin and tragedy is maintained, well-intended people can inflict a lot of damage upon Christ's church and upon their sisters and brothers. Bad things happen to people to whom the word *sin* does not apply.

If the gospel is as true and comprehensive as we claim, it will effectively address not only sin but also tragedy. It must be good news for the sinner seeking forgiveness and for the child of God living with surprising sorrows to which guilt does not apply. Christians who live with tragedy must hear a word of peace and hope, just as a sinner needs to hear a word of forgiveness and new creation.

Stan's Story

Four years out of seminary, Stan and his wife, Virginia, were doing well in their first pastoral assignment. They were respected in their small, Midwest community, especially by the young people. Stan and Virginia started a Saturday night coffeehouse ministry for teens. The congregation purchased a used bus for transporting children to Sunday school and for taking teens to various events.

Early one summer Monday morning, Stan and a group of teens, including some whose parents did not attend church, were scheduled to leave for a week of summer camp. As usual, some were tardy. So the bus pulled out of the parking lot late.

Stan and the excited bunch of teens had not gone more than a mile when he prepared to cross a set of railroad tracks he had crossed many times before. Visibility at the crossing was partly obscured by an embankment, and Stan approached the tracks with a high noise level in the bus. From the corner of his eye, he saw a train approaching. He hit the brakes, but the brake booster failed. Stan's legs were not strong enough to stop the bus in time. The train slammed into the front of the bus and dragged it more than two hundred feet before throwing it free.

When the bus finally stopped, it lay on its side, badly damaged. Most teens survived with minor to moderate injuries. But not sixteen-year-old Laura, who had recently begun attending the church. Laura's neck broke, and she died.

Stan was devastated. He had set out to take a group of teens to a place where they could grow in their faith and have a week of hearty fellowship. Now, instead, Laura was dead.

Laura's mother did not attend Stan's church. Her grief was deep and understandable. But she refused to believe Stan's account of the accident. She hired an attorney and sued Stan and the church for negligence.

In court, Stan could not convince the jurors that the brakes had failed. The judgment went strongly against him and the church. To make matters worse, some townspeople and church members turned against him. He was judged to be a careless driver.

Stan and Virginia never recovered from Laura's death, the senselessness of the accident, or the venom directed toward Stan in the aftermath. He had no way to vindicate himself; he was never invited to re-establish ministry in another congregation.

All of that happened fifteen years ago. For fifteen years, Stan and Virginia have lived with grief, shame, and suffering spawned by the accident, trial, and termination of ministry. They embody tragedy.

Deborah's Story

Never did a more chaste person enter a Christian college than Deborah. Bright, disciplined, and focused, she knew why she was there. Even as a child in a small, rural church, Deborah knew God had called her to be a missionary nurse. Though her parents could not provide much financial assistance, Deborah earned the bachelor of science in nursing (BSN) in four years, and at the top of her class.

While in school, Deborah fell in love with and married Philip, one of the most promising students on campus. He too had been called to be a missionary. The two of them served effectively for years in Latin America. They had two children. Deborah could have written a book on how wonderfully God leads.

In time, Deborah and Philip returned to their home country, where Philip began ministry as a member of the clergy in a prominent congregation. After a few years of effective ministry, Philip resigned. Weeks later, out of nowhere, he informed Deborah that he was homosexual and had been all his life. She was devastated.

Today, Deborah lives alone while Philip lives with friends who are also homosexual. Did Deborah do something wrong, somehow disobey God's will, to bring all this upon herself?

Nothing about Deborah's story would cause us to place blame on her. She believed she was obeying God by marrying Philip. But her world fell apart. Tragedy became her daily companion. Try as she might, Deborah has been unable to fix what was broken.

The Gospel and Tragedy

Can the gospel of Jesus Christ offer good news to Stan, Deborah, and many other Christians who identify with them? For the gospel to be good news to this broken world, it must include those visited by tragedy.

What, then, is the gospel's answering word? Jesus offers it in the following terms: "Come to me, all who labor and are heavy laden, and I will give you rest" (Matt. 11:28, RSV). His invitation is meant for all people, including those "heavy laden" by tragedy. Jesus doesn't promise to fix everything, only that he will give us rest. Reconciliation and restoration of family relationships, friendships, ministries, physical health, and/or effective service might or might not happen. In any event, Jesus's promise remains, "I will give you rest."

Because the gospel contains good news for Christians caught in the throes of tragedy, what should be the strategy for both speaking and hearing that good news?

First, until the kingdom of God comes in its fullness and the Father has put all things under Christ's feet (1 Cor. 15:25), we must, in complete honesty, face the fact that tragedy is no respecter of families, cultures, or churches.

Author Frederick Buechner, who has peered deeply into the Christian faith, challenges Christians to come to grips with tragedy and to find effective ways to address the gospel to it. Beneath our religion, he says, "We are all vulnerable to the storm without and to the storm within, and if ever we are to find true shelter, it is with the recognition of our tragic nakedness and need for true shelter that we have to start."[5]

More pointedly to clergy, Buechner says, "This is also where anyone who preaches the gospel has to start."[6] We have not fully preached the gospel when we address it only to problems that can be solved.

Confronting tragedy head on, giving it proper recognition, requires adopting a realistic view of life. Buechner knows that no matter the tragedy, God will perform his healing work in us. But, he cautions, the "sheltering word" of hope and resurrection cannot be spoken unless we have also paid honest attention to tragedy. Our "listening" is part of the "Christian word" we have to articulate. The "answering word," Buechner says, arrives "only after the [listening] word."[7]

Listening shows we too are vulnerable. It places us in the company of the Suffering Servant who has "borne our griefs and carried our sorrows" (Isa. 53:4, RSV) and who did not have a place to lay his head (Matt. 8:20; Luke 9:58).

Second, we must studiously avoid either trivializing tragedy by offering superficial solutions or using Scripture carelessly. For example, we can too easily reach for Romans 8:28 as a catchall explanation: "We know that all things work together for good for those who love God, who are called according to his purpose" (NRSV).

Sometimes well-intended people say this verse means that all the horrible things that happen to people finally turn out to be good in the end. Those who love the Lord will eventually see that all they thought was evil actually turned out to be "good in disguise." Others say if people will just be patient, evil will pass away and the good will replace it. Both explanations misrepresent the Romans text.

It is true that some things we thought were evil will later turn out to be blessings in disguise. It is also true that, by God's grace, many harmful things can be overcome and made to serve good purposes.

But Romans 8:28 does not say that in time all negative, harmful, and destructive occurrences will turn out to be good. The repeated sexual abuse of a child will never become good, no matter how much grace is eventually applied. Nor will a spouse who has suffered verbal and physical trauma wake up one day and conclude that it was all actually good. Sexual and physical abuse are grotesque crimes; they will never be anything else. God has no interest in calling good what is, in fact, evil.

Romans 8:28 *does* teach that no matter how bitter the memories, intense the evil, or sharp the pain, the redeemer God will work ceaselessly to achieve his good purposes in us. No evil can keep God from accomplishing this (Rom. 8:37–39). The creative work of our Redeemer neither ignores nor eliminates tragedy. Instead, in the power of Christ's resurrection, God works untiringly to show how new creation has the final word.

Third, the good news about Christ's resurrection is that it anchors our "eager longing" and hope of being set free from all bondage (Rom. 8:19–21, RSV). Tragedy, though baffling and oppressive, will not speak the last word for God's people and God's creation. To back up this certainty, the promised Holy Spirit now "seals" the guarantee of our inheritance (Eph. 1:13–14, RSV; cf. 2 Cor. 1:21–22; 5:1–5; 1 John 3:24).

Unlike the Greeks, who saw tragedy as a permanent element of life, Christians must not grant tragedy permanent residency in God's creation. It will finally be bracketed by fulfillment of God's eternal kingdom. Christian confidence is that "God will wipe away every tear" (Rev. 7:17).

Christians should live in hope and confidence as they stand before an empty tomb, rather than die in the Tombs with Bartleby.

THREE
THE GOD WHO HOLDS US

ON THURSDAY, March 16, 2001, forty-seven-year-old Kenneth Waters saw a cell phone for the first time, drank his first Starbucks coffee, and ate his first corned-beef sandwich in almost two decades. Waters had just emerged from eighteen years in prison for a crime he did not commit. His murder conviction was vacated by newly tested DNA evidence. Waters was raised in rural Massachusetts in a family of nine children. Prior to his arrest, he worked as a chef in a local diner.

As Waters emerged from a courtroom in Cambridge, Massachusetts, his exuberant family members, including some he had never met, hugged him.

"It's great to be free," he said.

One of the ecstatic relatives who greeted Kenneth was his sister, Betty Anne Waters. When, in 1980, Kenneth was convicted of murdering Katharina Brow, Betty Anne refused to accept the verdict as truth. Betty Anne's confidence in her brother's innocence changed the course of her life.

She was a young mother of two children who had dropped out of high school. She was so determined to exonerate her brother that she completed high school and entered college. Upon graduation, she was accepted into law school. Eventually Betty Anne became her brother's attorney and waged an extraordinary legal battle that led to Kenneth's release.

"There was no alternative," Betty Anne joked. "We were out of money for lawyers." She began writing to the New York-based Innocence Project and hunted down the old blood samples in her brother's case. With the help of another attorney and the Innocence Project, in 1999, Betty Anne asked that her brother's DNA be tested against the old blood samples. When the results came in, they did not match. Betty Anne and attorney Barry Scheck filed a motion for a new trial. Prosecutors agreed that vacating the conviction "would be in the interest of justice."

Betty Anne's commitment to proving her brother's innocence is both astonishing and inspiring. By the time she walked out of the courthouse on March 16, 2001, hand in hand with her brother, Betty Anne had spent eighteen years in unbroken service to him. What a covenant! She announced, "I don't think I've had a better day."[1]

Sadly, [Kenneth] Waters died in a tragic accident on September 19, 2001, only six months after he was released from prison… But Betty Anne Waters says of her brother's time after he was exonerated: "Kenny had the best six months of his life. After so many years behind bars, the world was new to him."[2]

Betty Anne's steadfast refusal to abandon her brother provides a beautiful window into understanding the meaning and character of Christian hope. The story can serve as a parable of God's unfailing love.

Christian hope is a central theme in the New Testament. The gospel and hope are inseparable. The apostle Paul calls God "the God of hope" (Rom. 15:13).

Individual or family crises, professional failures, physical suffering, depression, and abandonment by others can drain a Christian of all sense of hope. Despair, even resentment against God, can become one's companion. An inability to pray can feed one's sense of being abandoned by God. Frustration can displace peace and joy.

A friend of mine is a brain researcher whose special interest is serotonin. Serotonin is a neurotransmitter, a type of chemical that helps relay signals from one area of the brain to another. Serotonin plays an important role in human mood disorders. A low level of serotonin can cause a general feeling of despair marked by low self-esteem, pessimism, gloom, distrust, and cynicism.

If brain chemistry can have that much negative impact on a person's sense of well-being, how much more can the bruising experiences of life drain Christians of their sense of hope in the Lord? It can appear that all anchors have broken loose; nothing seems to hold. Frantic disorientation displaces hope. And God seems far removed.

If the Christian faith depended on how much territory our noble efforts and positive feelings could conquer, it would dissolve into a religion of works and arrogance for some, and of cringing failure for others. If Christian hope is something our personal accomplishments must anchor, forget it. The critical question is, *Do we hold Christian hope, or does it hold us?* Primarily, *do we hold God, or does God hold us?*

Let's return for a moment to Betty Anne Waters and her brother, Kenneth. Who held whom in their story? At times Kenneth probably flirted with the prospect of giving up. He must have often fought despair. Imagine sitting in prison for eighteen years, knowing you didn't commit the crime for which you were sentenced. There must have been lonely times when Kenneth fought hard to hold on.

But the key to Kenneth's release from prison wasn't what *he* held onto. It was who held onto *him*. In this remarkable story of love for a brother, Mary Anne held onto Kenneth as she fought weariness and he fought hopelessness. Clearly, Kenneth's holding on was of secondary importance. Had Betty Anne been less committed, Kenneth would probably still be in jail.

We often speak of Christians as having hope. In a secondary sense this is true, and our active participation should not be minimized. But, thankfully, we're not the primary authors of hope. In the New Testament, Christian hope is first of all a topic about who holds us. It has nothing to do with whether we *feel* hopeful. We may feel as though our spiritual serotonin is bankrupt. Nevertheless, we can still be firmly grounded in hope.

Good news! Christian hope springs from, and is anchored in, the resurrection of Jesus Christ. By raising Jesus from the grave, the Father unmistakably and irrefutably confirmed Jesus's witness to his Father. He also confirmed Jesus's claim that we are his friends, never to be forsaken (John 10:7–18; 17:6–19). To the sick, the lame, and people of disreputable character, Jesus announced the arrival of the kingdom of God (Mark 1:14–15).

> The Spirit of the Lord is upon me,
> because he has anointed me to preach good news to the poor.
> He has sent me to proclaim release to the captives
> and recovering of sight to the blind,
> to set at liberty those who are oppressed,
> to proclaim the acceptable year of the Lord.
> Luke 4:18–19, RSV

The formerly left-out ones gladly heard Jesus. Those judged the least likely candidates for the kingdom—even a tax collector for the Romans (Luke 19:1–10)—were given full citizenship by Jesus. Good news!

On Easter morning, by raising Jesus from the grave, the Father proclaimed, "Everything my Son has said about me and my kingdom is true." The apostle Paul summarizes: "For in him every one of God's promises is a 'Yes.' For this reason it is through him that we say the 'Amen'" (2 Cor. 1:20, NRSV).

Christian hope is the gift given by our heavenly Father on the authority of Jesus's life, death, and resurrection. Because of that authority, Christian hope can anticipate with absolute certainty that the kingdom our Lord inaugurated will be completed. Having Christian hope means being received into and supported in and by the future of our resurrected Lord (1 Cor. 15:12–28), who will never leave us or forsake us (Deut. 31:8).

To understand this, compare a monkey mother and a cat mother. When a monkey mother wants to move her babies, they must hold onto her for dear life. A safe journey depends largely on the ability of the babies to keep hanging on. But when a cat mother wants to move her kittens, she uses her teeth to take each by the scruff of the neck and carry it to a new resting place. A kitten may not "feel" like going, but it's off safely to new quarters anyway.

For ten days, sixty-six-year-old Tommy Hope of Hope Hull, Alabama, lay on the floor of his rural home after a fall that made it impossible for him to seek help. On the tenth day, Cissy Cartwright, who had been a letter carrier for twenty years, suspected that something was wrong. She noticed that Tommy had not checked his mail for several days. She went to the front door and called to Tommy, who communicated to her that he needed help. Cartwright entered the home and found Tommy dehydrated and injured. She dialed 911 and waited with him there in his home until an ambulance came.[3]

As inspiring as this story is, it does not define Christian hope, for clearly there was a perilous element of uncertainty in Tommy's situation. His hope could have gone unanswered.

Tommy Hope's situation is light-years away from saying, "My hope is in the resurrection of our Lord." The Christian's *future*, said theologian Karl Barth, is the *future* of something that has already happened—Jesus's resurrection. Paradoxically, the Alpha and the Omega, the beginning and the last, are the same—Jesus Christ.[4] The apostle Paul puts it this way: "The permanent [has] come in glory!" We can now live in "great boldness" (2 Cor. 3:11–12, NRSV).

One may be a child of Christian hope and at times feel hopeless, abandoned, defeated, depressed, and weak in faith. Even then, the God of all hope carries you.

The Trappist monk Thomas Merton (1915–1968) gave voice to the hope that holds us:

My Lord God,
I have no idea where I am going.
I do not see the road ahead of me.
I cannot know for certain where it will end.
Nor do I really know myself,
and the fact that I think I am following your will
does not mean that I am actually doing so.
But I believe that the desire to please you
does in fact please you.
And I hope I have that desire in all that I am doing.
I hope that I will never do anything apart from that desire.
And I know that if I do this, you will lead me by the right road,
though I may know nothing about it.
Therefore will I trust you always though
I may seem to be lost and in the shadow of death.

I will not fear, for you are ever with me,
and you will never leave me to face my perils alone.[5]

Knowledge of the God who holds us should affect our prayers. Ask the Lord to clear away our misperceptions about hope and to re-center our hope in the Good Shepherd. Then, in as elementary a form as necessary, simply begin to trust the God who holds us. The Holy Spirit will assist. Our first steps may be halting, but fear not! Prayer to the God who holds us is not a performance-based enterprise.

FOUR
TEXTS OF FRUSTRATION

F. B. MEYER (1847–1929), the famous British pastor who introduced D. L. Moody to churches in England, penned an insightful tribute to the Scriptures. He described the Bible as the storehouse of the promises of God. "It is the sword of the Spirit, before which temptation flees. It is the all-sufficient equipment of Christian usefulness. It is the believer's guidebook and directory in all possible circumstances."[1]

Through the ages, Christian teachers have given us many aids to prayer. But none compare with the holy Scriptures. Anyone who hopes to become a friend of God must become a friend of God's Word, the Spirit-enlivened story of God and his creation.

We speak of the books of the Bible as constituting the Christian canon. The word *canon* comes from a Greek word that means "measuring rod." As canon, the Bible is the church's measuring rod, the authoritative norm for what we believe about God and his will for creation. They are the Scriptures, the Word of God. They speak prophetically to every era and endure through the ages. Step by step, they fulfill their role in God's self-disclosure. The Scriptures speak in diverse, time-conditioned human voices. But those voices speak *for* another—for God. This is the church's conviction.

New Testament scholar Luke Timothy Johnson says the church's conviction regarding the Scriptures "can be expressed by the statement that the texts are 'divinely inspired,' for to speak of the Word of God is to speak as well by implication of the work of God's Spirit. Divine inspiration is one of the ways of expressing the unique authority of the writings of the canonical collection."[2]

The New Testament announces that Jesus Christ is God incarnate, come among us (John 1:14; Phil. 2:5–11; Col. 1:15–20; Heb. 1:1–4). He is God's definitive self-disclosure. He is the *Logos*, the eternal Word of the Father (John 1:1–5). Instead of the Jerusalem temple being the place where God dwells (destroyed 70 AD), Jesus's body is the "place" where God now dwells and where atonement for sin occurs (John 2:19–22).

Jesus, and the apostles, taught that he was the one to whom the Law and the prophets pointed (Matt. 21:42; Luke 24:13–27; John 5:39; Acts 10:43; 1 Cor. 10:4; 15:4; 2 Cor. 1:19–22; 1 Peter 1:10–12). In the Old Testament, said Martin Luther, we will "find the swaddling cloths and the manger in which Christ lies."[3] The Scriptures *become* the Word of God because of their faithful, Spirit-enlivened testimony to the God who encounters us in Jesus Christ (John 5:39). Before the two confused disciples who are walking to Emmaus on Easter can understand Jesus's resurrection, it is necessary for him to open the Scriptures (Luke 24:32), beginning with Moses and the prophets (Luke 24:27), and open their eyes in his breaking of the bread (Luke 24:30–31).

In the four Gospels, Jesus makes many glorious promises to his disciples. He promises them eternal life, never to leave nor forsake them, and to lay down his life for them. He promises the coming of the Holy Spirit, and to be with his disciples always, "to the close of the age" (Matt. 28:16–20, RSV). The apostle Paul says all the promises of God are fulfilled in Jesus Christ (2 Cor. 1:19–22). This truth is majestically affirmed by the apostle Peter: "[God's] divine power has granted to us all things that pertain to life and godliness, through the knowledge of him who called us to his own glory and excellence, by which he has granted to us his precious and very great promises" (2 Peter 1:3–4a, RSV).

Jesus's promises to his disciples, including the ones about prayer, are meant to be received and celebrated by the church of God. Their end is to glorify God, cultivate abundant life in God's kingdom, and equip us for service to the gospel. But the promises must be heard in context. Unless this rule is obeyed, much in the four Gospels can be confusing and frustrating. This seems particularly true of some texts that, on the surface, appear to be straightforward promises regarding prayer.

Let's examine some better-known texts of frustration. Hopefully, with the Spirit's assistance, these scriptures will convey the part of the gospel they were meant to illuminate. Instead of remaining texts of frustration, they will hopefully become texts of encouragement and consolation.

Texts of frustration are located in Matthew 7:7–8; 18:18–19; 21:22; Luke 11:5–13; 18:1, 6; and John 16:23–24.

To facilitate readability, the numerous commentaries used will not be specified at each point.[4]

The Matthew Texts

1. Matthew 7:7–11 (paralleled in Luke 11:9–13). "Ask and it will be given to you; seek and you will find; knock and the door will be opened to you. For everyone who asks receives;

the one who seeks finds; and to the one who knocks, the door will be opened" (Matt. 7:7–8).

These verses are part of Jesus's Sermon on the Mount (Matt. 5:1–7:27). The three imperatives—ask, search, and knock—express a confident attitude toward the heavenly Father's faithfulness. Jesus does not tell us what to request, what to seek, or that for which we are to knock. The object seems to be the "good things" of Matthew 7:11. No limitations or conditions are attached.

The three promises—receive, find, and open—seem to be equally unqualified. Regarding prayer, do the unqualified statements assure what they appear to guarantee? Is it really true that, no matter what, whatever one asks in the name of Jesus will be received?

If so, what should we tell Cynthia, who desperately prayed that her alcoholic husband would be saved? She asked, she sought, and she knocked on heaven's door until the day her husband died in a horrible head-on collision, having a blood-alcohol level that went through the ceiling. She read and believed Matthew 7:7–8. But the promises did not materialize. So for her, these verses have become a source of frustration.

Some scholars think these verses should be connected to the preceding ones in which Jesus warns against judging people who have "specks" in their eyes. Those passing judgment are said to have "planks" in their own eyes. These scholars say verses 7 and 8 teach that, rather than trying to remove the speck ourselves, we should ask God to do it. Having warned his disciples against judging others, Jesus exhorts his disciples to pray. If they pray in this way, their prayers for their neighbors will be heard. So, according to these scholars, Matthew 7:7–8 should not be received as unqualified promises for when Christians present requests to God.

Other scholars say there's no connection between Matthew 7:7–8 and the preceding and subsequent verses. They say verses 7–11 form a self-contained unit. Some scholars say that the "good things" promised in verse 11 refer to the eschatological (the end, or completion, of history and the kingdom of God) promises that accompany the presence of the kingdom of God. It is primarily about the work of the disciples in proclaiming the gospel. The "good things" promised could also mean the ordinary and ongoing needs of the disciples. God will supply their needs as they announce the gospel. Emphasis should be placed on God's faithfulness as the One who will provide for his people, not upon the requests themselves.

By either interpretation, we come to understand that the verses are not meant for selfish ends but always for God's glory according to kingdom interests. Matthew 7:7–8 tells us that the gifts from God commended in the Sermon on the Mount—righteousness, sincerity, humility, purity, and love—are available to Jesus's disciples when, in prayer, they *ask, seek,* and *knock.* For example, "Blessed are those who hunger and thirst for righteousness, for they will be filled" (Matt. 5:6).

In Matthew 7:7–11 Jesus is announcing the means for obtaining what is otherwise impossible. For example, Jesus tells a story in Luke about a tax collector who goes to the temple to pray. Unlike the Pharisee in the story, the tax collector stands at the rear and does not even look up to heaven. He beats his breast and says, "God, be merciful to me a sinner!" (Luke 18:13, RSV). True to the beatitude, God answers the man's prayer. Jesus says, "I tell you, this man went down to his house justified rather than the other" (Luke 18:14a, RSV).

2. Matthew 18:18–19 (see also 16:19). "Truly I tell you, whatever you bind on earth will be bound in heaven, and whatever you loose on earth will be loosed in heaven. Again, truly I

tell you that if two of you on earth agree about anything they ask for, it will be done for them by my Father in heaven."

The only condition stated in these two verses is that at least two people must agree about the request. Otherwise, the statement is starkly unqualified.

Then how should we answer Carl? Wilma is in heaven now, and Carl is alone. Wilma died of breast cancer last year. They joyfully served as lay missionaries in the Far East for twelve years. All during Wilma's illness, the two of them clung to Jesus's promise in Matthew 18, to no avail. If ever a set of promises belonged to anyone, Wilma and Carl thought, they belonged to them. In the name of Jesus they "bound" and "loosed."

Now that Wilma is gone, Carl doesn't want to be a missionary anymore. He is deeply puzzled, even disenchanted, over why Jesus's promises failed two missionaries who had freely answered God's call. How can we answer Carl?

First, note the context (vv. 15–20) in which the two verses appear. The subject of the context is church discipline, not promises regarding prayer. These verses provide instructions about how discipline should be administered in the church.

According to verse 17, when an offending member of the church will not listen to the group of two or three who have come to correct that person, the disciplinary matter should be brought to the attention of the church as a whole. If the offender refuses to repent, then he or she should be expelled from the church community.

In verse 18 the leaders of the church are given authority to "bind and loose" when attempting to maintain order in the body of Christ. Disciplining an unrepentant member carries the authority of the Lord. "Loosing" means forgiving; "binding" means retaining the punishment.

The promise in verse 19 that has given Carl so much trouble should not have been claimed as a promise for Wilma because the text deals with discipline, not petitionary prayer. The words "about anything" should be translated "about any judicial matter" regarding church discipline. The presence of Jesus is assured for the two or three who are brought together, namely the judges solemnly convened before the church and by the church, to render a decision. God's will stands behind the loosing and binding of verse 18. The strong promise is introduced to encourage the church in its administration of order.

In verse 19, Jesus continues to address church discipline as in the preceding verses. We know this because the initial word is "again." In this verse, Jesus reiterates what was said in verse 18.

The Greek word for *anything* is translated "every matter," or every church problem that requires discipline. The church leaders must ask for guidance from the Lord. Where two or three of them agree regarding the correct course of action, they can be assured of God's approval. What has been agreed to on earth in the matter of church discipline may be taken as the will of heaven. The church can count on the risen Christ for maintaining order.

3. Matthew 21:22 (paralleled in Mark 11:12–24). "If you believe, you will receive whatever you ask for in prayer."

"What could possibly be clearer?" Thelma asked as she listened to a preacher on television expounding this text. If ever God had spoken directly, she was sure she had heard his voice through this sermon. The preacher said, "The promise is meant for every child of God. God is bound by his word to honor his promise, with no reservations."

So Thelma confidently claimed the promise. She believed the little church she and her husband had helped support for many years would not close. In faith believing, she and Roy, who was now virtually an invalid because of rheumatoid arthritis, waited to see how God would save their church.

Two months prior, the last family who could provide any financial support moved to Dallas to find work, leaving Thelma and Roy alone on the Oklahoma plains. Two weeks ago, the responsible denominational official broke the bad news: The church would close. Nothing more could be done. The once thriving town had died.

The preacher on television would have served Thelma and Roy well if he had done more careful homework before preaching that sermon. Maybe he could have saved them from having serious reservations about God's faithfulness and worrying about where they went wrong. He had ripped the text out of context.

Verse 22 in Matthew chapter 21 must be placed within the context of verses 18–24. Matthew's version is shorter and more simple than in Mark 11:12–24. The larger context of the Matthew account is the passion narrative. In Matthew 20:17–19, for the third time, Jesus foretells his death.

In Matthew 21:1–11, we read of the events on Palm Sunday. In verse 12, Jesus enters Jerusalem, where he will be accepted by the blind and the lame but violently rejected by the Jewish authorities. Israel, in the form of those who control the religious establishment and who are politically influential, will reject Jesus. They will, finally, nail him to a cross.

As we know, Jesus does not normally go around cursing fig trees. But on this particular morning, as he is returning to the city, he is hungry. He sees a fig tree by the roadside, goes to it, and finds nothing. Then he curses the tree: "May no fruit ever come from you again!" (Matt. 21:19, RSV).

As often happens, the disciples miss the point. They are amazed over how quickly the fig tree withers. "Wow! Did you see that?" The meaning of what Jesus has done completely escapes them. The fig tree is a symbol of Israel's religious barrenness. God has come to Israel in the person of Jesus, and Israel is not prepared to receive him. Notice that Jesus's curse of the fig tree is preceded by his cleaning the temple and being indignantly rejected by the chief priests and teachers of the law (Matt. 21:12–17). Jeremiah 8:13 and Micah 7:1 use the fig tree as a symbol of Israel. Jeremiah speaks of Israel as a fruitless fig tree.

In spite of the disciples' rather irrelevant question about how Jesus has made the fig tree wither so quickly, Jesus honors their curiosity. So the subject changes from barren Israel to the faith that will keep the disciples from being powerless and barren like the fig tree. Israel's plight could, but doesn't need to, become the disciples' failure also.

In an effort to teach, Jesus gives a short sermon on the importance of faith. Emphatically, he tells his disciples that as they serve him in the kingdom, if they have faith, they will do what many think impossible. Recall that Jesus is about to leave his disciples and will soon entrust his ministry to them. He uses hyperbole, referencing a mountain, to make his point. His words are meant for instruction, not literal application.

Notice that "whatever" is conditioned by "you ask for in prayer." The effect of these words makes clear that granting requests is limited to the will of God (cf. John 14:13–14; 16:23). Prayer is Christian when governed by, "Thy kingdom come, thy will be done…"

Jesus is not promising his disciples magical powers to do whatever they please or to perform spectacular deeds, such as making fig trees wither. Everything must be indexed to the purposes of God. Matthew 21:22 points to the miraculous power available to Jesus's disciples in service to the kingdom, and for living fruitfully in anticipation of the Lord's return. Individual needs and petitions are certainly important, but they are not *all-consumingly* important.

After Mark's account of the fig tree and Jesus's instructions regarding faith and prayer, Jesus warns that we should not expect God to hear our prayers if we have not forgiven our neighbor (Mark 11:20–25).

The Luke Texts

1. Luke 11:5–13. "Then Jesus said to them, 'Suppose you have a friend, and you go to him at midnight and say, "Friend, lend me three loaves of bread"'" (Luke 11:5).

Early in life, Sybil believed that God had called her to the Christian ministry. Her minister, her family, and her friends all encouraged her. So she went to college and seminary to prepare, hoping to become the pastor of a congregation. After graduation, no doors opened for Sybil. One morning, as Sybil was reading the Scriptures, Luke 11:5–13 seemed to address her problem. She believed God would surely give to her what he had called her to do. She was sure God would be more responsive than the man who said to his neighbor, "Don't bother me." She knew her heavenly Father would give good gifts to her.

So Sybil went to the Lord in prayer. She asked, and she sought, but she did not receive, did not find. So she went on for further schooling to train as a hospital chaplain. Ten years after graduating from seminary, Sybil still has not been offered a place of pastoral service. She now wonders about her call and God's promises. Her confidence is waning.

Luke 11:5–13 follows the scene where Jesus teaches the disciples how to pray (the Lord's Prayer, 11:1–4). Only Luke preserves the parable. The verses present a striking contrast between a grouchy, reluctant friend and our loving, heavenly Father. These verses move us beyond the reluctant friend, who nevertheless assists his neighbor, toward the heavenly Father, who quickly and willingly gives to his children "fish" and "eggs" instead of "snakes" and "scorpions." He is eager to give good gifts to his children.

The section takes us back to the Father of the Lord's Prayer. Verses 5–13 actually form a commentary on the Lord's Prayer. The purpose of the parable is to lead us to the heavenly Father. It encourages us to pray the Lord's Prayer with confidence. In agreement with the language of the Lord's Prayer, God will respond to our needs as we lay them before him. Even more than friends who come through for us in spite of inconvenience, our heavenly Father will respond more readily and richly.

However, some Christians read these verses and conclude that the Father has offered his children an open and unlimited checkbook. They treat God like a parent or grandparent who, without considering other values, would tell a child, "You want it? You have it."

Verses 9–13 explicitly state the contrast between the friend and the Father. "So I say to you: Ask and it will be given to you; seek and you will find; knock and the door will be opened to you" (Luke 11:9). God's greatness should not keep us from approaching him (Heb. 4:14–16). He isn't too busy running the universe to quickly respond to his children.

The Lord's Prayer says, "Give us each day our daily bread" (Luke 11:3). Verses 9–13 tell us how and in what measure God will answer our daily petitions. Not only will the Father respond; he will also give only good gifts to his children. The verses are meant to tell us what the heavenly Father is like, even as the Lord's Prayer has already done. The disciples should be bold in their requests.

Those who see this text principally as promises for material things need to read more carefully. "Daily bread" is certainly included in the promise. But the most important promise, that for which the children of the Father should hunger most, is the gift of the Holy Spirit.

The conclusion, "How much more," is frequent in rabbinical literature. It accents the point that if something is true in a small instance, how much more will it be true in the larger case? If we, being evil, know how to give good gifts to our children, then "how much more" will God give good gifts to his children! But the most important *more* is the Holy Spirit, whom the Father will give to us. The Spirit is far greater than all earthly gifts.

We must not miss the point that the promises, though including material things, find their highest fulfillment in the gift of the Holy Spirit. The Spirit will make it possible for God's children to live as citizens of God's kingdom. The Spirit will plant in God's children the life and power of the kingdom. For this, the children should rejoice most. The Spirit is the Father's highest gift. So why not request that gift above all others? (See Rom. 15:13–19.)

Luke 11:5–13 presents an intimate picture of the relationship between God and his children. God urges us to approach him in intimacy and with confidence. The verses must be firmly grounded in the Lord's Prayer, where Jesus teaches his disciples the fundamental attitudes of prayer. *First,* they must have a concern for God's character and honor, and a desire to see him overcome evil. *Second,* they must subject all their individual interests and petitions to an overriding hunger for the kingdom of God on earth, even as it has come in heaven. *Third,* Jesus's disciples should guard God's honor and always pray in a way that will display God's glory. *Fourth,* in addition to, and more urgent than, requests for basic material provisions, Jesus's disciples should pray for forgiveness and spiritual protection. In asking for forgiveness, they are required to forgive others. Disciples who want to honor God will do so by the way they live in dependence upon the Father.

2. Luke 18:1–8. "Then Jesus told his disciples a parable to show them that they should always pray and not give up" (Luke 18:1).

This parable and Jesus's explanation is one of the most difficult of all the texts of frustration. It is similar to Luke 11:5–13. It tells us God will not long delay helping his children who call upon him. As in Luke 11:5–13, Jesus contrasts the willing God with a human who is reluctant to help those who call for assistance. But in this parable, the contrast is even stronger. The figure with whom God is contrasted is not a reluctant friend but "a judge who neither feared God nor cared what people thought" (Luke 18:2).

Here is a man who is used to ignoring requests. One day a widow, a person with little or no political clout, comes to the judge. She requests justice against someone who has wronged her. Given his habits, the judge has no inclination to pay attention to this woman, who occupies a low rung on the social ladder. But she does not give up easily. She keeps coming back again and again.

Finally, wearied by her persistence and realizing she will not desist, the unjust judge caves in. "Give that woman anything she wants. Just keep her quiet!"

In sharp contrast to the unjust judge, Jesus speaks of God, who is both just and loving. How much more quickly will God grant justice for his chosen ones, "who cry to him day and night? Will he delay long over them? I tell you, he will vindicate them speedily" (Luke 18:7–8a, RSV).

If ever Jesus's words should encourage Christians to expect God to act quickly and always to relieve the anguish of his people, they should do so here, right? If an unjust judge can finally be moved to execute justice, how much more faithfully and immediately will God act?

We would be dishonest not to admit that, in instance after instance, this simply does not happen. Early Christians died while being torn apart by wild animals in Roman arenas. Others were burned at the stake, or were cooked alive, while bound to a red-hot iron chair. Days before the Allies liberated his prison camp, the Nazis hanged Dietrich Bonhoeffer (April 9, 1945), thus ending the life of one of the world's most promising Christian leaders. Today, Christians in the Middle East are dying at the hands of Muslim extremists (ISIS). Some Christians suffer physically and emotionally, obscured by forced silence, praying for relief that doesn't come.

"And will not God bring about justice for his chosen ones, who cry out to him day and night? Will he keep putting them off? I tell you, he will see that they get justice, and quickly" (Luke 18:7–8a).

What are we to say? The apparent contradiction between Jesus's words and what many Christians endure seems to speak for itself. One explanation that is sometimes offered must be rejected: Jesus's parable of the unjust judge is meant to toughen his disciples. He wants them to be tenacious when offering their petitions to God. Increase Christian fortitude by persistently storming heaven! But that's not at all what the text says. Jesus *contrasts* the willing heavenly Father with the wicked and resistant judge.

Frankly, commentaries don't resolve all the questions this text raises. But they can help.

E. Earle Ellis (*The Century Bible*) says that Luke is apparently writing to a situation in which Christians are enduring severe persecution, a crisis in the church. The persecution may be so great that some are denying their faith. The Christians are "crying to God day and night" for relief from persecution.

Jesus's promise to his disciples should be understood as an eschatological promise. This means that the text involves consummation (fulfillment) of God's kingdom at Christ's second coming, the *parousia*. Then the suffering saints of God will be vindicated. Those in the parable who call out to God symbolize the church as it waits for Christ to be revealed in all his glory. By this interpretation, Christ is assuring persecuted disciples that the Father will not long delay his Son's triumphant return. Commentator John Pollard says that the word *quickly* does not mean "immediately." *Quickly* has to do with God's faithfulness. The church can count on this, whatever the age or situation.[5] Others maintain that the Greek word means "suddenly."

One of the most stirring appeals for the Lord's return and the vindication of the saints appears in Revelation 6:9–10. When the Lamb opens the fifth seal, John sees under the altar the souls of those who have been martyred for God's Word and for their testimony. They cry out, "How long, Sovereign Lord, holy and true, until you judge the inhabitants of the earth and avenge our blood?" (Rev. 6:10).

This interpretation of the text might be supported by Jesus's haunting question in Luke 18:8: "However, when the Son of Man comes, will he find faith on earth?"

Unfortunately, scholars do not agree on the interpretation offered.

The John Text

John 16:23–24, NRSV. "On that day you will ask nothing of me. Very truly, I tell you, if you ask anything of the Father in my name, he will give it to you. Until now you have not asked for anything in my name. Ask and you will receive, so that your joy may be complete."

What could be plainer or more straightforward than this? Could we fault anyone who takes the Lord at his word and asks confidently in his name? "In my name" is the only limitation the text appears to attach to the promise. It seems to urge Christians to petition the Lord for relief from all hindrances that keep them from thriving as Christian parents, spouses, pastors, laypeople, businesspeople, and so on. A person simply needs to request "in Jesus's name" and should confidently expect his or her prayers to be answered.

If the "anything" someone has petitioned in Jesus's name doesn't follow, obviously God has defaulted on the promise. Neither he nor we should be surprised if frustrated, disillusioned, and angry people are left in the wake.

Some time ago, a pastor in Florida made such a promise to his congregation. He urged members to tithe on the basis of what, in the Lord's name, they wanted to earn as an annual income. The more the people earned, the more they could give to the church, he contended.

A contractor followed the pastor's instructions and promptly went bankrupt. Angry and "defrauded by God," the contractor sued the church—not being able to reach the Lord. But the judge threw the case out of court, saying he didn't know how to subpoena God.

Jesus's words, "Ask anything of the Father in my name, and he will give it to you," seem to be on the pastor's side. But again, the text can easily be abused if taken out of context.

What help can commentaries offer?

First, let's establish the larger context. This text forms part of Jesus's farewell discourse that runs from John 14:1 through 17:26. None of the other Gospels have anything quite like this. The farewell discourse provides an interpretation of Jesus's completed work on earth. It also teaches the relation of the risen and glorified Christ to the believers (14:1–31), and the believers' relation to the world

(16:1–33). We learn of the pattern of the Christian life in 15:1–27. Prominent in the farewell discourse is the promise of the Holy Spirit (14:2–17, 25–27; 16:4–15). The farewell discourse is followed by Jesus's high-priestly prayer (17:1–26).

The text of frustration in 16:23–24 is part of the farewell discourse where Jesus teaches what a Christian's relationship to the world should be. In verses 16–24, Jesus says that the pain over his death will give way to joy in his resurrection, which will result in Christ's abiding presence through the Holy Spirit.

Verses 16–18 may refer more directly to Jesus's post-resurrection appearances (chapters 20–21) than to the Holy Spirit's coming. At any rate, Jesus has already assured his disciples that he will not leave them as orphans (14:18). He will come to them in the person of the Holy Spirit. Although for us, who live on this side of Easter and Pentecost, all of Jesus's words seem clear, we have to put ourselves in the puzzled disciples' place. They have not seen the rest of the story yet when Jesus is speaking in this passage.

So the tone of this text is established by Jesus reassuring his disciples when he is about to depart. He prepares them for his death (John 16:16) and for the good things to follow. At first they will be like a woman in labor. But afterward they will rejoice that a child has been born (16:20–21). They have pain now but will soon receive a joy no one can take away.

Then comes the promise that may spark frustration. "On that day you will ask nothing of me. Very truly, I tell you, if you ask anything of the Father in my name, he will give it to you. Until now you have not asked for anything in my name. Ask and you will receive, so that your joy may be complete" (John 16:23–24, NRSV).

Taking into consideration what Jesus has been trying to tell the disciples, "on that day" refers primarily to the time after Jesus's resurrection, maybe to after he has ascended and the Holy Spirit has descended. Commentators are not sure what meaning we should give to "ask nothing of me." Does it mean, "You will ask me no questions," or, "You will ask me for nothing," meaning favors? On the surface it seems to contradict the next sentence, where Jesus encourages the disciples to ask. "Ask nothing" may mean not ask a question or not ask for a gift.

The best interpretation is that, after the resurrection, the disciples will not *need* to ask for further information from Jesus. They will then have all the information they need because the Holy Spirit will teach them everything. The Spirit will remind them of all Jesus taught (14:26). Jesus has already promised that the Holy Spirit will lead the disciples into all truth (16:13).

"I tell you the truth" usually introduces a new thought. The asking at the end of verse 23 appears to be different from the asking at the beginning of the verse. But an alternative view is that the whole verse deals with prayer. If this is what verse 23 is about, then Jesus is saying that prayer will be directed toward the Father and not toward himself. In either case, the events about to unfold will bring changes.

After Jesus's resurrection, the disciples will direct their prayers to the Father, who, in Jesus's name, will give them "whatever" they ask. Jesus places no limits upon what the Father will give. The purpose for all this is birth of the disciples' joy. They will go through trials (16:33), but as they place their trust in God, he will establish joy in the disciples' hearts. Joy is connected with prayer, the purpose of which is to complete the disciples' joy. Joy can be made complete only through prayer.

The requests John has in mind in 16:23–24 are not primarily for the ordinary needs of life. The promise doesn't rule out material blessings and/or physical healing. But such things are not the principal subject of the promise. When understood as ordaining a shopping list, the text is mistreated. Rather, the promises are intended to provide whatever enriches eternal life and makes the Holy Spirit's work more fruitful. These are things for which all followers of Jesus should ask. They may be assured their requests will be granted. Christians should pray for the fullness of Christian joy. As they ask, they will receive (John 16:24).

Conclusion

The explanations of the texts examined in this chapter are not meant to discourage anyone from taking petitions to our heavenly Father. We are God's children. God invites us into his presence. But when appealing to Scripture as the basis for our petitions, we must remember to treat Scripture carefully, considering that the context may change what we think we see, and may also lead to an expanded understanding of God's Word. By using good study tools, we can avoid superficial reading and safeguard the respect the Scriptures require for understanding.

Above all, even in our most careful study, only the Holy Spirit can make the Bible the living Word of God. The Spirit must enliven Scripture just as the Spirit must enliven Scripture's readers. The following prayer can help guide us:

Blessed Lord, who hast caused all holy Scriptures to be written for our learning; Grant that we may in such wise hear them, read, mark, learn, and inwardly digest them, that by patience and comfort of thy holy Word, we may embrace, and ever hold fast, the blessed hope of everlasting life, which thou hast given us in our Saviour Jesus Christ. *Amen.*[6]

FIVE
IN DEFENSE OF FAITH THAT COMPLAINS

Six years ago, with assistance from a micro-business loan, Angelica began a pandesal-making business in her metro-Manila barangay, or neighborhood. Pandesal is bread commonly eaten at breakfast. Because of the quality of both her product and her customer service, Angelica's business has grown steadily.

Six months ago, she became a born-again Christian. Since then, problems have developed. Her husband, who had sporadically assisted in her business, strongly resented her conversion.

Three weeks ago, Angelica's husband stalked out in anger and hasn't been seen since. Because of competition from a new, full-service grocery that recently opened within sight of her bakery, Angelica's sales have nosedived, making it difficult to repay her loan and provide for her three young children, one of whom has been discovered to have juvenile-onset diabetes.

Not one to respond to problems passively, one morning while trying to pray, Angelica unleashed a fierce complaint against the Lord.

"Why is it, Lord," she vented, "that, since I became a Christian, much of my life seems to be going downhill? Are you even paying attention to me? Do you even know my children and I are here?"

One Perspective

Seen from one perspective, it appears the Bible is ready to correct, if not rebuke, Angelica. Serving the Lord and complaining against the Lord seemingly can't live together peaceably in his presence.

Many psalms give voice to untroubled faith. For example, there isn't a ripple of unrest in the often quoted twenty-third psalm. And who could imagine storm clouds ever gathering above the one who declares, "The LORD is my rock, and my fortress, and my deliverer, my God, my rock, in whom I take refuge, my shield, and the horn of my salvation, my stronghold" (Ps. 18:2, RSV).

In the New Testament, the gospel of Luke opens with sterling models of unwavering faith surrounding the birth of Jesus—Zechariah and Elizabeth, Joseph and Mary, and Simeon and Anna. In the gospel of John, Jesus tells his disciples, "Do not let your hearts be troubled. You believe in God; believe also in me" (John 14:1). The apostle Paul's prayer for the Christians in Rome echoes Jesus's assurance. "May the God of hope fill you with all joy and peace as you trust in him, so that you may overflow with hope by the power of the Holy Spirit" (Rom. 15:13). The eleventh chapter of Hebrews is known as the Bible's Hall of Faith. It is lined with glimmering statues of saints who possessed and consistently exhibited untroubled faith. None of them—Abel, Enoch, Noah, Abraham, Isaac, Jacob, Joseph, and others—showed a sign of ever doubting the Lord. The book of Hebrews is a brilliant pastoral reprimand for Jewish Christians who were in danger of giving up their faith and returning to their Jewish beliefs and practices.

Scriptures such as these could easily drive a troubled Christian like Angelica into guilt and immobilizing despair.

A Closer Look

But is this the complete picture? Does it do justice to both the Old and New Testaments? A closer examination reveals that complaint has historically played a vital role in the faith journey of God's people. Furthermore, troubled faith is even welcomed into the precincts of worship. At first, it might strike us as strange that God, who superintended the writing of the Scriptures, would permit a powerful minority report to remain. Why allow the people of God to challenge God's faithfulness as a sworn covenantal partner?

We might expect that, if complaint language is found in the Bible, it will certainly be confined to the Old Testament as an expression of inferior, pre-Christian faith. But what if, upon closer examination, we were to discover such language in the New Testament? Such a discovery would strongly challenge any one-sided picture of unruffled faith and confidence. And a pathway for bold, honest, and comprehensive understanding of faithful prayer would be opened.

By permitting complaint to play a prominent and unedited role in Scripture, might God be telling us something important about himself, even about how God identifies with us?

Two Kinds of Complaint

In the Bible we find two kinds of complaint. One is condemned. The other is not.

The first kind is associated with "murmuring" (Hebrew, *aw-nan*). It journeys in the company of disobedience and unbelief. Taken alone, its consequences are enough to suck the breath out of all complaints.

After the children of Israel receive the Law during their stay at Mt. Sinai, they begin a march toward the Promised Land. A few days into their journey they began to complain "in the hearing of the LORD" about their misfortunes. The Lord's anger blazes. Fire falls from heaven and destroys some outlying parts of the camp. Undeterred, the people continue to pine for the good ol' days in Egypt and complain about not having meat to eat with their manna. While the Lord's anger blazes, Moses, thoroughly disenchanted and overworked, seeks to wash his hands of the entire venture (Num. 11:1–15).

Later, Moses sends twelve spies into Canaan to examine the land and assess the Israelites' prospects for a successful invasion. Eleven spies give a report so dispiriting that the people rise up against Moses and Aaron. The Israelites complain bitterly, and declare en masse their preference for having died in Egypt. In response, God declares that because he has endured ten episodes of "complaint" riddled by disbelief and disobedience, all males above twenty years of age (with the exceptions of Caleb and Aaron) will perish in the wilderness, never to enter the Promised Land (Num. 13:17–14:38; 32:6–16).

In the New Testament, complaining or murmuring is usually associated with unbelief, disobedience, or conflict. The scribes and Pharisees often complain about how Jesus is conducting his ministry (Luke 5:17–21, 29–32; 15:2). The citizens of Jericho "murmur" because Jesus goes home with Zacchaeus (Luke 19:7, RSV). In another instance, an unnamed woman empties expensive contents of an alabaster box on Jesus's head. Some who watch complain indignantly. What a wasteful deed! The perfume should have been sold and the money given to the poor (Mark 14:3–5).

In the sixth chapter of John, some of the more than five thousand people, whom Jesus taught and fed with bread and fish the day before, murmur rancorously (vv. 41–42, RSV) as Jesus begins to speak of himself as the bread of life (v. 35). In outraged disbelief, they abandon Jesus en masse (v. 66). In the epistles, Jude excoriates a group of rebellious false teachers in the church. He labels them "grumblers, malcontents [who follow] their own passions" (v. 16, RSV). They are loudmouthed, opportunistic boasters who exploit the gospel for their own benefit. Their complaints are condemned.

A second type of complaint is known in the Old Testament as "lament." The Hebrew verb form is *'abal*, to mourn or lament. This word is not associated with unbelief or disobedience. In fact, lament plays an essential role in Israel's faith. Usually appearing in poetic form, laments are a particular kind of prayer and constitute a major part of Israel's petitionary prayer. Laments appear in various parts of the Old Testament. One-third of the book of Psalms is written as lament. An entire book, written in response to the destruction of Jerusalem by the Babylonians (587–586 BC), bears the name Lamentations.

Laments arise within a context of assumed mutual covenant. Mutual fidelity is the bond. God's people are bound to him in faithfulness, and he to them. Hence, Israel has a right and obligation to insist that God prove himself faithful in specific ways.

Some laments are expressed as petition, in the voice of an individual who speaks from within an intimate, personal relationship with God. He or she prays as a member of the community. Life's disruptive experiences—pillage by an enemy, famine, illness, isolation, exile, imprisonment—can evoke a petitionary lament. The entire community, not just an individual, may be confronted with the prospects of annihilation. The faithful people of God do not passively acquiesce to such crises; they lament.

When the Babylonians destroy Jerusalem and the temple, Israel laments: "O God, why have you rejected us forever? Why does your anger smolder against the sheep of your pasture?" (Ps. 74:1).

In harsh and impatient language—in the context of worship—they inform God, "O God, the nations have invaded your inheritance; they have defiled your holy temple, they have reduced Jerusalem to rubble." Israel does not hesitate to inform the Almighty that they "are in desperate need" (Ps. 79:1, 8).

Usually, laments begin as protests in response to a perceived discrepancy between how God has promised to act and how matters are actually unfolding. Nevertheless, they are prayers of hope, of faith, not eruptions of unbelief and rebellion. Laments are uttered in confidence that God will both hear and act in response. So, ironically, laments are expressions of faith voiced in full-throated candor and urgency, not in polite, garden-party phrases. They aren't designed to be indulgent compliments.

Characteristically, laments are passionately realistic. They address God in forceful, daringly assertive, even abrasive language. They can even be "savage in their urgency."[1] As we saw in chapter 1, the prophet Habakkuk charges God with silence and fear in the presence of the invading Babylonians. He effectively requires that God stop hiding like a coward, that he stand up and begin acting like the God he claims to be! (Hab. 1:1–4). Who among us would address God that way? And, to think, God permitted such a book to be in the Bible.

Remarkably, while laments may begin with forceful protest against how God seems to be acting (or not acting) under dire conditions, normally they "end in praise, celebration, and confidence that God has acted or will act."[2] The *petition* in Psalm 13:1–4 is matched by *praise* in verses 5 and 6. *Resolution* in Psalm 22:22–31 follows *lament* in 22:1–21. However, in some laments (e.g., Pss. 39 and 88), there is no positive resolution. In such instances, an admirable candor recognizes that not all prayers are automatically or quickly answered. However, even the absence or postponement of resolution is contained in the context of God's faithfulness.

Laments may express guilt and ask for forgiveness, but normally they testify to having been loyal to the Lord. They petition a corresponding loyalty from him. Laments are prayerful "acts of hope, uttered in confidence" that God will hear and bring about a good resolution.[3]

Walter Brueggemann and Christopher J.H. Wright both comment significantly on the absence of lament in Christian worship. They say omitting lament deprives us of an important part of faith. It is as though, Wright says, we have "airbrushed great swaths of the Bible from our consciousness." The absence leads us to "smother" parts of our lives that should be part of our praise. We are left to "pick up our sufferings" on our way out of church.[4]

The Parable of the Frog

In *Pilgrim at Tinker Creek*, Annie Dillard describes frogs jumping along Tinker Creek in the summer. The jumping and croaking frogs thrilled her. Then she saw a frog lying still, partly in and partly out of the water. As she watched, it slowly crumpled. The spirit disappeared from its eyes. It shrank like "a deflating football." The tight, glistening skin on the frog's shoulders rumpled and fell. "Soon, part of his skin, formless as a pricked balloon, lay in floating folds like bright scum on top of the water." It was, Dillard wrote, monstrous and terrifying. Annie "gaped bewildered, appalled."[5]

What happened to the glistening frog? A giant water bug ate it. It sucked out the frog's insides.

For years, Dillard's riveting account of the empty frog has been, for me, a parable of the conditions that give rise to lament among God's people. Crises of life tumbling in from many directions and in many forms can drain spiritual and physical energies and wrinkle our faith, as the water bug did to the frog in Tinker Creek. Examined from the surface, members of the fellowship of lament often appear to have things under control. They may even feel urged by some members of their faith community to report their victories—what appears on the surface. But below the surface, they're nearly being pulled under by personal, familial, emotional, or professional crises. Their eyes dulled, their faith cratered, they've almost sunken in like the empty frog.

As we have seen, the Old Testament church does not nervously cram lamenters into the closet, close the door, and try to forget them. The God of Abraham, who made a place for lament in Israel's worship and in its Scriptures, is truly astonishing!

Jesus's Lament and Ours

Jesus, as the incarnate Son of God, faithfully believed the promises of Scripture were being fulfilled in him. Nevertheless, during the Lord's final testing on the cross, he engages in lament! Matthew tells us that at "about three in the afternoon, Jesus cried out in a loud voice… 'My God, my God, why have you forsaken me?'" (Matt. 27:46).

From depths plumbed and comprehended only by our Lord and his heavenly Father, in this dark hour, the Son of God reaches into Israel's storehouse of laments, into the wealth of Israel's tested faith, and voices one of the most abrasive, accusatory laments from the Old Testament, Psalm 22. He speaks aloud only the first part of the first verse, but the next twenty-one verses may course through his anguished mind and body, from "Why are you so far from saving me" to "save…my afflicted soul from the horns of the wild oxen!" (RSV). In no other moment in Jesus's life are the recorded words of the epistle to the Hebrews more applicable: He was "made like [Abraham's descendants]…in every way, in order that he might become a merciful and faithful high priest.... Because he himself suffered when he was tempted, he is able to help those who are being tempted" (Heb. 2:17–18).

It may be difficult to believe Jesus was truly tempted in all points, even as we are. But his lament on the cross incontestably witnesses to the fact. The cross is not a divine charade, staged to overawe onlookers. There, God is truly taking upon himself the abyss—the bottom depths—of human suffering, sin, and abandonment. In Jesus's lament we are permitted a look at what Roman Catholic theologian Romano Guardini calls the "frightful intensity" of Jesus's union with us, and his absorbing God's "ultimate odium," his abhorrence of our sin.[6] God is truly "disarming" all the powers that might have successfully stood against him (Col. 2:15).

Jesus's lament can help us better understand the incarnation. In him, God really did become one with us. He really did bear our burdens, even the burden of faithful complaint. He identified with Angelica and thereby answered the question of whether a child of God can legitimately express faithful complaint. If Jesus can cry out, "Why have you forsaken me?" then all God's children can do the same from their depths of testing.

Jesus's lament, like all true faithful complaint, is actually an expression of profound faith in God. Like the psalmist in Psalm 22, Jesus is confidently calling upon his heavenly Father to be as faithful as Jesus believes him to be. "My God, my God" means, *Be faithful to yourself, O Lord.* Or, *Be who I believe you are.*

As strange as it may seem, Jesus's lament is an expression of praise, of worship. In advance of his resurrection, while still in the depths, Jesus, like the psalmist, believes his Father will show his strong arm of redemption.

In the Old Testament, we observe that usually a resolution to the crisis of faith follows the lament. God proves himself faithful.

This pattern characterizes the second part of Psalm 22 (vv. 22–31), from which Jesus quotes while on the cross. Has the Father provided a resolution for Jesus's lament? Has he powerfully answered his Son? Has he justified his Son's confidence? Yes!

Easter morning—the resurrection of our Lord, the empty tomb—is the Father's answer. By his sovereign power, the Father, through the Holy Spirit, raises Jesus from the grave (Rom. 6:4; 8:11; Eph. 1:20; Col. 2:12; 1 Peter 3:18). What seems to be abandonment is not that at all. It is the unveiling and perfecting of the mystery of salvation proclaimed and celebrated throughout the New Testament (Eph. 1:3–14; 3:7–13; Col. 1:26–27; 1 Tim. 3:16) and throughout eternity by the church of the living God (Rev. 7:13–17; 15:1–4).

Through new creation, by the Spirit, we partake in Jesus's resurrection. No matter the depths of our laments—our prayerful complaints—the same God of power who raised Jesus from the grave is now working in us (2 Cor. 13:4; Eph. 1:15–23).

Yes, Angelica, even in the midst of your complaint, you, a child of God, are being carried on the shoulders of our Great Shepherd, held in the bosom of the Father, and are being "transformed into [Christ's] image with ever-increasing glory…" (2 Cor. 3:18). The New Testament Christians are not strangers to severe testing. But transcending it all lies a hope that already knows that the future will look like the risen, reigning, and coming Lord. Christian hope is singularly warranted by the resurrection of Jesus Christ (Rom. 5:2–5; 8:34; 15:13; 2 Cor. 4:18; Eph. 1:18; 1 Peter 1:30).

So, "precious Lord, take my hand, lead me on, let me stand. Through the storm, through the night, lead me on to the light. Take my hand, precious Lord, lead me home."[7]

SIX
INTERCESSORY PRAYER

The Challenge of Intercessory Prayer

Perhaps no dimension of prayer presents a greater challenge to many thoughtful Christians than intercessory prayer. From the human side, intercessory prayer involves pleading or making a request to God on behalf of another, or for resolution of problems that transcend human capacities. To intercede is to intervene.

The Bible contains many instances of intercessory prayer. Jesus is the Great Intercessor (Heb. 7:25). The Holy Spirit intercedes before the Father for Christians (Rom. 8:26–27). Both the Old and New Testaments show that God expects his people to pray prayers of intercession. The Bible records instances in which prayers of intercession accomplished their intended purpose (Num. 12:1–16; 14:1–20; Acts 12:1–19) and instances when it didn't. For example, Paul asks the church in Rome to pray for the success of his planned work in Spain (Rom. 15:23–33). Unfortunately, he never actually makes it to Spain.

On the surface, the definition, the divine invitation (Matt. 18:19–20; James 5:14–16), and the procedure for intercessory prayer seem to be straightforward and accessible. God's people petition him for something good that only God can accomplish. Then, being the holy, responsive God of sovereign love and power that he is, assuming that the request pleases him, God acts, and the request is granted, all to his glory and the increase of his kingdom.

For many Christians, however, human experience and careful reflection generate obstacles that can turn intercessory prayer into a frustrating puzzle. Prayer becomes an occasion for conflict and disappointment rather than victory and peace. Intercessory efforts seem to disappear into a void. An offered explanation, "Well, God always answers prayer in some way, even if you don't recognize it" doesn't satisfy. It simply intensifies the pain.

This experience can be particularly painful when a person hears stories about how God complied with some other intercessor's petition. *Why him and not me?* is an understandable question. Does God play favorites? Does God have "on" and "off" days?

If God is all knowing and all loving, if he is the living God who always acts faithfully, why should he need to be coaxed and informed by finite creatures? Is such a God worthy of the name *God*, or of worship by intelligent people? And if the sovereign and unchanging God does what he wants to do in his own time and in his own way, then what sense does it make to say he is moved to action by intercessory prayer?

The Bible clearly commends intercessory prayer as occupying an important place in our walk with the Lord (Isa. 62:6; Eph. 6:18; 1 Tim. 2:1–2). But for many, before the commendation can be obeyed, questions regarding the intelligibility and meaning of intercessory prayer must be addressed. Otherwise, some Christians will leave intercessory prayer to others and respectfully pass by on the other side.

Additional Questions

First, if the sovereign and unchanging God does what he wants to do in his own time and in his own way, what sense does it make to say he is moved to action by intercessory prayer? How presumptive!

Second, if God possesses an infinite and eternal perspective, if he has a plan for completing his kingdom, then the absurdity of creatures trying to tell the Creator what he should be doing becomes glaringly obvious.

And besides, doesn't the Bible discourage this kind of "nonsense"? Listen to the apostle Paul as he instructs the Roman Christians about God's will for Israel: "But who indeed are you, a human being, to argue with God? Will what is molded say to the one who molds it, 'Why have you made me like this?' Has the potter no right over the clay?" (Rom. 9:20–21a, NRSV; see also Isa. 29:16; 45:9; 64:8; Jer. 18:6).

Someone may answer, "Well, we're just urging God to do what he already knows to be best." But would we daily call the fire department to remind firefighters they need to respond to alarms as they come in? Would we call a mother to remind her to protect her children? How pointless, then, to remind God to get on with the business of being God.

Third, the notion of God changing his mind in response to intercessory prayer is highly troubling for some. What are the implications for a God who changes his mind at the request of finite creatures? Can that kind of God be trusted to follow through on promises and plans? Imagine the chaos in the divine life and world order if, in response to multiple intercessory prayers, God were to be preoccupied with which requests for a change of mind to honor and which ones to ignore.

One of the best known instances in the Scriptures of God appearing to change his mind is found in Exodus 32. The Israelites have sinned by worshiping a golden calf and have subsequently engaged in an orgy of drinking, eating, and playing. God becomes very angry with them (Ex. 32:7–10). He is so angry he decides to exterminate them (Ex. 32:10; 1 Cor. 10:6–10).

But Moses intercedes for the rebellious people. He even chides the Lord for being overly angry! "Why does your wrath burn hot against your people?" (Ex. 32:11, NRSV). Next, Moses explains to the Lord that if he obliterates the people, God's reputation with Pharaoh and the Egyptians will suffer. So Moses counsels God to turn away from his dreaded plan. God seems to consider Moses's words. "Then the LORD relented ["repented," KJV] and did not bring on his people the disaster he had threatened" (32:14).

Does God actually change his mind as the text seems to indicate? Does God regret something he purposed while in a divine huff? Does he then arbitrarily restructure his course of action?

Actually, the text means that God revises his course of action ("the Lord repented"), not as a fickle and mercurial deity but in a manner consistent with his sovereign, steadfast purpose. The Hebrew word *nacham* can mean "to be moved by pity, to have compassion."

Is There Anything Better?

Have we exhausted all options for understanding intercessory prayer? No!

We have noted that the New Testament calls us to practice intercessory prayer. The book of James is a good illustration. "Is anyone among you in trouble? Let them pray. Is anyone happy? Let them sing songs of praise. Is anyone among you sick? Let them call the elders of the church to pray over them and anoint them with oil in the name of the Lord. And the prayer offered in faith will make the sick person well; the Lord will raise them up" (James 5:13–15).

Martin Luther was correct: "The Lord is great and high, and therefore he wants great things to be sought from him and is willing to bestow them so that his almighty power might be shown forth."[1]

Some wise Christian teachers are ready to lead us into a rich and defensible understanding that transcends the objections raised earlier.

First, let's eliminate magic. Theologian John H. Wright says that when speaking of intercessory prayer we must reject any explanation that sounds like magic. Magic tries to manipulate powers greater than human power and place them under human control.[2] Once in control, a person can gain what is wanted.

The language may *sound* Christian, but if prayer is used, even unintentionally, to gain control over God, then that kind of prayer is nothing more than sub-Christian magic. One may even pray "in the name of Jesus" and still be engaged in magic. God becomes a manipulative tool for obtaining self-centered and shortsighted goals. The Christian magician assumes the role of deity. God becomes a genie who must obey. True worship, which places the glory and will of God far above all else, ceases.

Too often, unsuspecting Christians snatch up books on prayer or attend seminars that contain little more than magic—no matter how well intended. Amazingly, a book that sold millions of copies and cemented the adherence of many readers declares that "seeking God's blessings is our ultimate act of worship."[3] The author was oblivious to his subtle and dangerous substitution of self for worship of the sovereign, triune God, who—to know in radical trust and obedience—is life eternal. This author's exposition of one Old

Testament prayer was sealed against any broader and conditioning biblical context.

The Bible completely rejects any notion that we should cage God to serve our interests. Under no condition should one attempt to place God under powers or any law external to his sovereign freedom. To do so is blasphemy. Wise children of God will have nothing to do with this.

The Lord's Prayer makes clear that all prayer begins and ends in worship. We place ourselves before God as sacrifices of praise and service (Rom. 12:1–3). Theologian Donald Bloesch says, "In all Christian prayer the overriding motivation is to glorify God and to discover his will for our lives."[4]

The acceptable posture for all Christian prayer is love, praise, trust, and thanksgiving. Christians who pray this way will avoid the error of using prayer to try to constrain God or to guarantee engineered results.

Second, consider the apostle Paul, who often encourages Christians to pray. He surprises us by saying we don't even know how to pray. No Christian should approach God as if he or she has everything figured out. Instead, Paul says, we should recognize our limitations, our "weakness," as he puts it. To pray aright, Christians must pray "in the Holy Spirit." They pray with recognition that, in Jesus's name, the Holy Spirit takes our sincere but limited petitions and presents them to the Father. The Holy "Spirit helps us in our weakness. We do not know what we ought to pray for" (Rom. 8:26).

Paul's instruction inspires confidence and submission to God's will while sucking all oxygen out of presumption and self-will.

Third, as John H. Wright reminds us, the first condition of intercessory prayer is faith.[5] In the New Testament, faith means radical trust in, and submission to, the God who by grace alone justifies and reconciles sinners. Faith involves completely turning away from reliance on our own righteousness, wisdom, craftiness, and strength. It means holding steadfastly to God.

The New Testament teaching assumes the person who approaches God is in right relationship with the triune God *and* his or her neighbor (Matt. 5:23–24; James 4:1–12). Prayer is offered in the name of Jesus and "in the Holy Spirit" (Jude v. 20). The Holy Spirit makes the riches of Christ available to us. The Holy Spirit connects us to Jesus (Rom. 8:9–11). The Holy Spirit is the risen Lord's gift to all who believe in him (John 7:37–39; Acts 2:38). The Spirit alone makes it possible to call out, "Abba! Father!" when we address God (Rom. 8:15; Gal. 4:6). The Spirit also joins Christians to the body of Christ—to its Head (Christ), and to their Christian sisters and brothers through grace (1 Cor. 12:13; 2 Cor. 13:14; Eph. 4:3–4).

Fourth, Wright reminds us that if we pray guided by the New Testament, we don't pray alone. Through the covenant of Christ's shed blood, we are each children of God. He calls us by name. But we're also members of Christ's body, the church. As such, we are members one of another (Rom. 12:4–5; Eph. 4:14–16; Col. 3:14–16). We're before God as sisters and brothers of each other and of Jesus Christ. They are God's gifts to us, and we to them. We're privileged and commanded to "carry each other's burdens and in this way" to "fulfill the law of Christ" (Gal. 6:2). To pray as Christians is to pray for the good of Christ's body, for its life and ministry everywhere.[6]

We still have the freedom and urgency to offer our petitions. When a child is critically ill, we would expect a Christian parent to appeal to the Lord for help. But our needs and the needs of those near us should not become our all-consuming interest. If this happens, prayer becomes introverted and myopic, a series of disjointed lists shipped to heaven, unrelated to any larger work the Lord is doing. Intercession should be kindled far more by a longing for God to complete his kingdom among us.

The gospel of Christ redirects us toward something larger than ourselves, toward the coming of the kingdom of God in Jesus Christ. The gospel by no means eliminates the individual who is the subject of new creation (2 Cor. 5:11–21). But it does set us free from slavery to self-centered living; it sets us free to pray and work for God's peace on earth.

Fifth, as Donald Bloesch explains,[7] God takes his people seriously. They are his covenant partners. He does not sit outside human history, alone in sovereignty. Instead, he engages in the messy process of life. A God who doesn't take his people or events seriously simply is not the God of the Bible.[8] God's very name, "I AM," or "I AM WHO I AM," or "I will be whoever I will be," explains Old Testament scholar Timothy Green, means, "He is the God whose very character is gracious presence. This unique God is not the Zeus of Mount Olympus who waits for the worshipers to come to where he is in order to worship him. He is the God who accompanies [journeys with] his people"[9] (Gen. 26:24; 28:15; Ex. 3:12; Josh. 1:9; Isa. 43:2; Jer. 30:11; Matt. 28:20; Acts 18:9–10).

"Covenant" means that the free, triune God has entered a bond with us. His sovereignty is astonishingly manifest and his purposes achieved in the risks of love. God, who—as triune—is already a community of love, invites us into community with him through our Lord Jesus Christ. Is this beyond our comprehension? Yes, as much as God's wisdom and knowledge are "unsearchable" (Rom. 11:33).

Unlike the dead idols that Isaiah and Jeremiah ridicule (Paul calls them "mute," 1 Cor. 12:2), the God of the Bible listens. He answers. He is the living God. Karl Barth said, "Prayer exerts an influence upon God's action, even upon his existence. This is what the word 'answer' means."[10]

Old Testament scholar Walter Brueggemann succinctly stated the covenantal and dialogical character of Israel's prayer.

Prayer in the Old Testament is an interactive conversation—a drama, a dialogue—in which both parties [Yahweh and Israel] have a role. Its defining premise is the character of YHWH [Yahweh] who is characteristically known as and trusted to be the one named in the great doxologies and memories of Israel. . . . Prayer is thus an activity that has as its characteristic premise the reality of covenant in which these two parties have sworn enduring allegiance to each other.[11]

Brueggemann adds that the dialogue between Yahweh and Israel "is open to every issue that may occur in human life," for the God of covenant "is relevant to and adequate for every circumstance."[12]

In covenantal mutuality, both the divine and human partners add something essential; both God and we, God's children, are enriched. Deny this, and relationship becomes a meaningless, one-sided term. To say prayer influences God has *everything* to do with mutual, covenant love, and *nothing* to do with coaxing, cajoling, controlling, or manipulating God.

Never forget that in this covenant relationship, God remains God. It is he who makes the covenant possible. As a covenantal partner, God is absolutely trustworthy. We know this because he is always faithful to himself. He never fails to be who he is—the triune God of holy love. As Christians, we know this because the heavenly Father was faithful to himself by being faithful to his Son. He suffered with his Son. And, by the Holy Spirit, he raised our Lord from the grave on the third day. Jesus is the New Covenant. Therefore, we also know God will be faithful to complete the kingdom Jesus inaugurated.

On this basis, Bloesch tells us, "Prayer is not simply petition, but strenuous petition. It is not just passive surrender, but active pleading with God. . . . It consists not merely in reflection on the promises of God, but in taking hold of these promises."[13]

Intercessory prayer does not set out to change God's purposes. Instead, beyond all human explanation, out of a divinely initiated partnership, intercessory prayer helps empower and accomplish God's purposes. Call this "filial reciprocity."[14]

Intercessory prayer unleashes God's purposes on earth, even as they are in heaven.[15] William Law said prayer is a mighty instrument, "not for getting man's will done in heaven," but "for getting God's will done on earth."[16] Striving with God in intercessory prayer helps us discover the broader scope of God's will.

Fulfillment of God's will on earth is at least partly contingent on our prayers. Bloesch says, "There are several ways in which God's will can be implemented, and through prayer we seek to discover the best way."[17]

If this is so, intercessory prayer becomes the Christian's great privilege, calling, and responsibility. It is a great thanksgiving to the God who has made a covenant with us in Christ. Christians certainly don't overpower God. Rather, as we prevail in intercessory prayer, so does God. We're covenant partners who work with him for the coming of the kingdom on earth. What a high calling as sisters and brothers of Christ![18]

The apostle Paul uses the language of warfare to articulate this high calling and responsibility. "Our struggle is not against flesh and blood, but against the rulers, against the authorities, against the powers of this dark world and against the spiritual forces of evil in the heavenly realms" (Eph. 6:12).

If all of this seems to pass human understanding, then remember that so do the actions of the gracious God. In grace, through intercessory prayer, God *takes us on as his working, contributing, junior partners.* Through the prayers of the saints, God acts to accomplish his purposes in the church and the world. In freedom, God binds himself to his people's prayers. Intercessory prayer opens to us God's resources for witness, for struggling against "the spiritual forces of evil" (Eph. 6:12), for spiritual discernment (1 Cor. 2:14), and for ministry.

John Calvin believed that God advances his kingdom through the prayers of his people and overthrows the powers of darkness. Understood in this way, intercessory prayer is work, hard work, faithful work, kingdom and vineyard work. The work of intercessory prayer also includes participating in Christ's sufferings (2 Cor. 1:5; Phil. 3:10; 1 Peter 4:13). It includes suffering with the God who suffers over his broken world.

Indulgent and self-centered people will not be found in these precincts. Elsie Gibson observed that many of us are so impatient that our greatest likelihood of failure lies in giving up because God does not jump to do what we want.[19]

Sixth, a final part of explaining intercessory prayer involves a description of the church as given by the apostle Peter. He calls members of Christ's church "a chosen race, a royal priesthood, a holy nation, God's own people" (1 Peter 2:9, NRSV). That designation is used for the people of Israel in Exodus (19:6, NRSV). Now, Peter says that mission belongs to the church, the new Israel built upon Jesus Christ, the "living stone, rejected by men but in God's sight chosen and precious" (1 Peter 2:4–6, RSV).

What does it mean for Christians to be priests? An important role of Old Testament priests is to bless the community (e.g., Num. 6:24–26). Actually, they dispense or pronounce God's blessing, God's grace, God's name upon the covenant community, but more broadly "upon all people regardless of culture, language, creed, or ethnicity."[20] Priests know God is the life giver. But he has made them "a means or vessel of God's life-giving grace…they partnered with him as a dispenser or instrument of that grace."[21] Astonishingly, to speak of Christians as priests of God ("a royal priesthood") means that from the Father, by his Son, and through the Holy Spirit, God has made Christians chosen associates in the divine-human partnership of which Christ is the head and we are the body. That is the calling, privilege, and responsibility our Lord extends to all his children.

What can intercessory prayer do? It can open heaven. It can open prison doors (Acts 4:1–31). It can renew the intercessor's spiritual life. Intercessory prayer can cast out fear. It strengthens Christian ministers and missionaries. It can serve the aims of redeeming grace in the world. It can unleash revival in the church and launch missionary movements. It can overcome oppressive regimes and establish justice in the land. It can break down walls of racial, ethnic, gender, and age discrimination. Intercessory prayer can do this in societies and in individuals.

The question is not what God is willing to do or whether God takes us seriously. The question is, To what level of intercession is the church of Christ willing to commit?

Marjorie Suchocki succinctly summarizes: "God works with the world as it is in order to bring it to where it can be. Prayer changes the way the world is, and therefore changes what the world can be. Prayer opens the world to its own transformation."[22]

If intercessory prayer is so rich, why are some parents' prayers answered while the prayers of others seem not to be? Why does intercessory prayer by one spouse result in a healed marriage, while the prayer of another does not? Why does a stunning revival of faith break out in China but not in Great Britain?

These questions and others raise the problem of tenacious and persistent evil in the world.

SEVEN
THE MYSTERY OF INIQUITY

A VIDEO shows twenty-one-year-old Dylann Roof entering Emanuel African Methodist Episcopal Church in Charleston, South Carolina, on Wednesday evening, June 17, 2015. The senior minister, Reverend Clementa Pinckney, was conducting the Wednesday evening prayer meeting. Roof sat down and listened to part of the service. Then he stood up, pulled out a .45-caliber handgun, and proceeded to murder nine people, including Rev. Pinckney, who was also a highly regarded South Carolina state senator.

Before Roof began his massacre he spewed his hate, saying he was there to "shoot black people. You rape our women, and you're taking over our country. And you have to go."[1] Some victims were: a recent graduate of Allen University; a thirty-one-year veteran of the Charleston County library system; a university enrollment counselor; the coach of the girls' track team at Goose Creek High School; and a retired director of a Community Block grant program.

Roof brought with him not only a gun he should never have been legally allowed to purchase[2] but also a troubled past that included poor school performance, a broken home, and a record of multiple arrests for drug possession and trespassing on the grounds of a shopping mall from which he had been banned. The nation reeled over the magnitude of the massacre and wondered how a twenty-one-year-old could have descended to commit such unspeakable evil.

This massacre brings us to what many Christians feel is their most obstinate obstacle to prayer: the reality of unrelenting evil in a world where God has supposedly placed all things in heaven and earth under the reign of his risen Son.

The New Testament claims that all powers, visible or invisible, are made to serve the ascended Lord (Eph. 1:15–23; Phil. 2:9–11; Col. 1:19–20; 2:13–15; 1 John 3:8). But many Christians observe how sin and the powers of darkness continue to destroy families, corrupt nations and political officials, and plow the lives of women and children under an international sex-trafficking industry. Christians are deeply troubled by apparent contradiction between the New Testament claims regarding a victorious Christ and the character of his heavenly Father, and what they experience and observe in the world.

While some Christians seem able to skip over this apparent conflict, others cannot. Inability to live with or to resolve seeming contradiction hobbles prayers and faith. They simply don't know how to pray confidently and intelligently when evil, in its many forms, seems so powerful. Sometimes they pray for evil to be put to flight in their families, and it seems that Christ answers prayer. In other equally urgent instances, nothing seems to happen. Evil continues to advance. Spousal abuse continues. A son commits suicide. And the ancient Christian community in parts of the Middle East all but disappears at the hands of religious fanatics.

For many Christians, rather than feeling confident they are praying to the One who rules over the powers, it seems more like they're playing a random, cosmic lottery where the outcome is uncertain. In our prayers, are we just taking our chances, hoping for the best? Win some, lose some?

Such language may seem abrasive, even faithless, to some. To others it is honesty compelled by the obvious. God's sovereignty certainly seems to be in question, or intermittent, at best.

We can choose to avoid raising such questions. We can maintain aloof stability and unrattled confidence. But such stability and comfort come at the price of leaving behind many sincere Christians whose prayers, faith, and actions have been immobilized by the tenacity of evil.

Attempting to protect Christian faith against hard questions, or offering answers that trivialize questions, succeed only in making faith irrelevant for many people.

Chomp or Lights in the Trees?

Author Annie Dillard spent a year at Tinker Creek observing the natural world. She repeatedly faced a question: What is nature's truth? Are beauty, design, and purpose nature's truth? Or does the truth of nature finally turn out to be "chomp, crunch"—destruction?

Does the world lead us to conclude that a wise and purposeful Creator authored it? Or does the world finally force us to conclude that it is purposeless, mindless waste? The evidence Dillard offers so insightfully in *Pilgrim at Tinker Creek* seems hopelessly mixed.

For example: You're a female ichneumon wasp (an insect with worm-like larvae that are parasites in or on other insects). You have mated, and your eggs are fertile. Your young will starve if you can't find a caterpillar on which to lay your eggs. You know that, when the eggs hatch, the young will eat any creature on which they find themselves—including yourself! So, if you can't find a caterpillar to dump them on, you must broadcast the eggs over the fields. The eggs will hatch, and your young will starve. "You feel them coming, and coming, and you struggle to rise."[3]

Or consider the female lacewing. Lacewings are fragile, green insects with large, rounded, transparent wings. Sometimes when a female lacewing lays her fertile eggs on a green leaf, she becomes hungry. She stops laying eggs momentarily, turns around, and eats the eggs she has just laid, one by one. Then she lays some more and eats those too.[4]

But Dillard has also seen nature's beauty. She has been struck by its unfathomable intricacy.[5] "Do you know," she asks, "that in the head of the caterpillar of the ordinary goat moth there are two hundred twenty-eight muscles?"[6] She sees that nature is not a rough sketch but is, rather, "supremely, meticulously, created, created abundantly, extravagantly."[7]

When surgeons learned how to remove cataracts, they operated on people across Europe and North America who had, since birth, been blinded by cataracts. Many tested their patients' sense of perception of space both before and after the operations. After the bandages were removed from the eyes of a little girl, she was then taken into a garden. Astonished by what she saw, she stood speechless in front of a tree. As she gazed into the branches, with sunlight streaming through, she joyously exclaimed, "The tree has lights in it!"[8]

Dillard searched for "the tree with the lights in it" through a peach orchard in summer and the forests in the fall. Then, one day as she walked along Tinker Creek, she "saw the tree with the lights in it. I saw the backyard cedar where the mourning doves roost charged and transfigured, each cell buzzing with flame.... It was less like seeing than like being for the first time seen, knocked breathless by a powerful glance. The flood of fire abated, but I am still spending the power." Because of what she saw, her left foot shouted, "Hallelujah!" and right foot answered, "Amen!"[9]

Like many Christians, Dillard is perplexed over the tension between what she believes about a loving God who created and governs the world, and the galloping moral and natural evil she observes. Honesty requires that she not deny the conflict. She thinks she can detect this tension in the Old Testament. Walter Brueggemann agrees, even though the tension is not as pronounced as Dillard suspects.

The Old Testament evidences a strong conviction that moral consistency characterizes God's dealings with God's people and creation. Confidence that the obedient receive God's blessings while the disobedient receive God's curses is "everywhere present in the faith of ancient Israel" (summarized in Deut. 30:15–20).[10] Nevertheless, this confidence is often placed in jeopardy by inescapable observations that disobedient people often seem to flourish while obedient people languish. Life's chilling evidence is that "no trustworthy connection exists between covenant-keeping, commandment-obeying obedience and covenant curses or blessings."[11] Some courageous voices sound the observed dissonance. Resolutely, Jeremiah asks God, "Why does the way of the wicked prosper? Why do all the faithless live at ease?" (Jer. 12:1). Not to be outdone in courage, Job confronts God with a similar question: "Why do the wicked live on, growing old and increasing in power?" (Job 21:7).

Like the Old Testament saints, says Dillard, we too "are permitted to have dealings with the Creator," and we too must ask questions about God. Is God a God of "chomp" or a God of "lights in the trees"? Nature provides inconclusive, even contradictory evidence.

The beauty Dillard has seen might be "the cruelest hoax of all."[12] Much of what Tinker Creek offers "buoys" her. But much "drags [her] down."[13]

As Christians we must look elsewhere.

As we move from Tinker Creek into the world of human affairs, questions about God and the world intensify. We'll soon encounter innocent children brutalized by drug-addicted parents and infants born with heroin addiction and alcohol syndrome. Move further, and we'll learn that in 2015, somewhere "between 21 million and 30 million men, women, and children [were] enslaved" as a result of labor or sex trafficking. "There are more slaves now than during all the years of the entire transatlantic slave trade combined."[14]

Olga, a nineteen-year-old Moldovan, is one of these. "For more than a year she has been held as a sex slave in . . . western Macedonia." When Preston Mendenhall interviewed her secretly, she suffered from an infected puncture wound on her right breast, inflicted by a client during "a fit of sexual rage." Olga lacked access to the most basic medicine that might help treat and heal her wound.[15]

All of this, mind you, in a world where Christians teach that the kingdom of God was inaugurated in the person of Jesus Christ, as promised in the Scriptures. Might we have some sympathy for those who become confused by the apparent discrepancy between Christian claims and powers of individual and corporate evil?

Christ the Victor?

The horrors of millions currently enslaved in labor or sex trafficking clash headlong into New Testament claims that the risen and ascended Christ now reigns over the powers and principalities of this age. Hear anew what the New Testament says Christ accomplished on the cross: "He disarmed the rulers and authorities and made a public example of them, triumphing over them in it" (Col. 2:15, NRSV).

This means that the crucified, resurrected, and ascended Christ has taken evil powers captive. He has stripped them of their armor. Their humiliation is a grand display of our Lord's victory (Eph. 4:1–10). How expansive is the claim for Christ's victory? The Father has placed his ascended Son "far above all rule and authority and power and dominion, and above every name that is named, not only in this age but also in the age to come. And he has put all things under his feet and has made him the head over all things for the church, which is his body, the fullness of him who fills all in all" (Eph. 1:21–23, NRSV; see also 1 Cor. 15:27).

But, if this is true, why do habitual spouse and/or child abusers and slave traffickers still ravage nations and families? To make the problem even more troublesome, the powers and principalities seem to acquire the characteristics of a sinister kingdom or aggressive empire. Consider "the unstoppable march of the tobacco giants" that "take advantage of lax marketing rules in developing countries" to aggressively sell cigarettes "to new, young consumers." In 2009, the developing world's share in global cigarette sales climbed to a whopping 76 percent.[16]

"If current smoking patterns continue, 7 [million] of the world's 10 million annual deaths from tobacco in 2025 will occur in developing countries."[17]

The Grace that Sees Differently

What should Christians believe and do in the face of militant and undeniable evil? How should we answer what seems an observable fact that not all things have been put under our Lord's feet?

What we should do, says Annie Dillard, depends on what we see. There is a "seeing" that involves a "letting go."[18] The secret of seeing, she says, "is the pearl of great price."[19] Her words echo Jesus's parable of the merchant who sold everything to gain the "pearl of great value" (Matt. 13:46, NRSV). He let go of everything because of what he had just seen. The apostle Paul tells the Corinthian Christians essentially the same thing. What an unbelieving world sees as real is, in fact, transient and illusory. The truth, power, and mystery of the gospel are "eternal" (2 Cor. 4:18; see also 1 John 5:10). But this eternal view can be seen only through the enlightenment and power of the Holy Spirit (John 3:1–15; 1 Cor. 2:8–14).

Theologian Hendrik Berkhof has spelled out the implications of what Christians must see.

First, Berkhof says, Christian must see that, in the crucifixion of Jesus, the powers of evil and their enmity toward God are fully and forcefully exposed. They have been outed, unmasked, their cover blown (Eph. 6:12; Col. 2:14–15). "They can no longer exist without being forced to uncover their true nature and thereby to abandon their role as gods and saviors."[20]

They have not only been exposed as overt and destructive in the broader world of human affairs, but they also work deceitfully inside Christ's church (2 Cor. 11:14; 2 Peter 2:1–3, 10–22; Jude vv. 17–23). James exposes them in graphic language (2:1–12; 4:1–13; 5:1–6).

Part of the church's calling is, in the power of the Spirit, to identify the powers and principalities, wherever they operate, and declare to them "the manifold wisdom of God" (Eph. 3:10).

Second, Berkhof says that not only has evil been fully exposed, but also, on the cross and in Jesus's resurrection, God terminates evil's boast that, through the fear of death, it can freely run amok in God's creation (1 Cor. 15:54–57; 2 Tim. 1:8–10; Heb. 2:14–15). Its self-crafted license has been forcefully revoked. Anyone who knows the true Word of God, and the devil, who is a liar, Karl Barth assures us, can have nothing less than "complete certainty" regarding the victory of the former.[21]

After playing their strongest hand, by moving others to crucify Jesus, the powers of hell fail miserably. In obedience to the Father, Jesus takes upon himself the sin of the world on the cross, absorbing the worst blow hell can deliver. He does not fold and does not flee, though some taunt him (Luke 23:35). On Easter morning the Father, through the Spirit, pronounces a sovereign *Amen!* to his Son's witness (1 John 5:9–10).

The end for the "god of this world" (2 Cor. 4:4, NRSV) has come, his doom sealed—no matter how much commotion he causes on his way out. To paraphrase the theologian Karl Barth, the battle has been won decisively; now the mopping-up campaign needs to be completed. The struggle will be temporary, and there will be no armistice or treaty with the adversary.[22]

"It is finished" (John 19:30). "Come and *see* the place where he lay. Then, go quickly and *tell* . . ." (Matt. 28:6b–7a, emphasis added). "Hallelujah!" (Rev. 19:1). As threatening as the struggle often seems to be, it is the "sum of folly and futility. Satan can place no army in the field that is more than a vacuous threat."[23]

This is what the apostle Paul, Hendrik Berkhof, and Annie Dillard all want us to see. Dillard says that, because she has received abundant grace (John 1:16–18; 1 Peter 1:1–2), she need not "sulk along" the rest of her days "on the edge of rage."[24] Her right foot now shouts, "Hallelujah!" and her left foot answers, "Amen!"

Suffering with a Suffering Christ

"What are Christians to do?" we ask.

"That depends on what they see," we answer.

Another part of *doing* needs to be included—suffering with Christ in an unfinished world. If Christ is suffering in the world to complete his kingdom, then surely Christians must be with him, must suffer with him, by acting justly and loving mercy (Mic. 6:8).

Paradoxically, joy and suffering are two sides of the same Christian coin stamped HOPE (Luke 9:23; Rom. 8:22–25; Phil. 3:7–14; Col. 1:24; 1 Peter 4:13). As Christians, we live between the *already* and the *not yet* of the kingdom (Matt. 13:31–33; Phil. 3:12–16; Heb. 2:8–9; 1 John 3:2). In this between time, we are called to share the sufferings of Christ (1 Peter 4:13; Phil. 3:10–11). In so doing, intercessory prayer and the faith that works through love reach their highest expression.

EIGHT
WHEN GODS FAIL

Scarecrows in a Cucumber Field

God remains; *gods* collapse. They fail. That's a central message in the biblical books of Isaiah and Jeremiah. Using razor-sharp language, these prophets eviscerate all forms of idolatry practiced in Judah and the surrounding nations. They lampoon the lifeless gods to which people pray. Idols must be nailed down tightly to keep them upright! By contrast, Isaiah and Jeremiah praise the Creator God. They speak of him as the living God who imparts life to all but does not draw his life from the world.

With brief exceptions, in the closing years of Judah's existence, idolatry eats like acid through Judah's identity as people in covenant with God (Solomon's kingdom divides into two nations, Judah and Israel, in 922 BC). Readers of Isaiah and Jeremiah are usually dismayed over the tenacity of idol worship. The practice embeds itself deeply into Judah's soul. How pervasive is idolatry? Jeremiah answers: "Your gods have become as many as your cities, O Judah;

and as many as the streets of Jerusalem are the altars you have set up to shame, altars to burn incense to Ba'al" (Jer. 11:13, RSV).

Relentlessly, Isaiah and Jeremiah work to convince kings and people that idolatry is a deceptive and fruitless practice, leading only to religious death and national ruin. Jeremiah describes idols as "scarecrows in a cucumber field. . . . there is no breath in them" (Jer. 10:5, 14, RSV).

As a child, I observed that once crows realize it's a scarecrow they're up against, they alight in droves. They see that the scarecrow has no power in itself—only the power crows are willing to grant. Ironically, the blind people of Judah aren't that perceptive.

Isaiah and Jeremiah lampoon artisans who make idols and those who worship them. In one account, Isaiah uses humor to show the absurdity of idolatry. He tells of an idol maker who selects a tree in the forest, waits for the tree to mature, and cuts it down. The idol maker burns one half to warm himself and cook a meal. He takes the other half back to his workshop and laboriously shapes the wood into a human form. Then he places his creation in a shrine, bows down, and says, "Save me, for you are my god!" (Isa. 44:17, NRSV).

The foolish idol maker is too blind to see he could just as easily have burned the half he now worships. Isaiah's devastating conclusion is that, when the man worships the idol, he "feeds on ashes" (Isa. 44:20).

Jeremiah and Isaiah never tire of pointing out that powerless idols don't carry their worshipers; the worshipers carry their idols (Isa. 45:20; 46:1–2). In time, idols, their makers, and their worshipers collapse in confusion (Isa. 44:18–20).

Judah's idols fail. They break down under the weight of national crises. As people are preparing to go into Babylonian exile after the destruction of Jerusalem (587/6 BC), they load their idols onto "weary animals" (Isa. 46:1, NRSV). The broken-down gods can rescue no one; they too are forced into exile. That, Isaiah and Jeremiah say, is what always happens to gods.

The God Who Does Not Fail

In contrast to idols, the God who created the heavens and the earth will carry his people—in good times and in bad. Unlike idols, God isn't part of the finite world. God is the One beside whom there is no other. He is the living God, the Redeemer. God doesn't have to be rescued in times of distress, bouncing along on the backs of fleeing worshipers (Isa. 46:2).

Unlike idols, God is the source of his own life. Many people in Jerusalem think no enemy nation will ever destroy the temple because then God will be defeated. They foolishly think God is much like a pagan deity who depends on a temple or a nation for existence. The prophet Ezekiel slams the brakes on that notion. He tells the people that even if Judah and Jerusalem are destroyed, God will live on. Even without a temple, and even if his people are taken captive, the living God will continue to direct the course of history. In astonishing language, Ezekiel actually describes the glory of the Lord abandoning the temple (Ezek. 10:1–22; 11:22–25; 12:8–19).

From our safe distance, it's easy to applaud Isaiah and Jeremiah's judgment against Judah. We wonder how those foolish people could have been so blind as to worship the lifeless products of human hands. No wonder their prayers failed! Along with the prophets, our righteous anger rises to defend the eternal God.

But hold on! The temptation and practice of trusting gods that eventually collapse does not end with the last verses of the Old Testament. Jeremiah's warning to Judah is equally applicable to us: "Do not learn the [idolatrous] ways of the nations" (Jer. 10:2).

Isaiah and Jeremiah say the gods will always fail because they cannot hear or answer. In the end, all such investments become insolvent. Idol worshipers will have to wearily load their dumb idols onto a beast of burden and follow them down the road "into captivity" (Isa. 46:2).

Let's face it: Prayer fails for many of us because we bow before gods of our own making instead of the free, true, and living God who inhabits eternity. Will we permit the Holy Spirit to expose the gods to whom we pray and who can give back only what we have given to them? Will we let the living God smash our gods?

In *The Screwtape Letters,* Screwtape, an old demon, instructs his nephew, Wormwood, regarding how to defeat his "patient" (a new Christian). Wormwood should not worry that his patient is praying. Wormwood should just make sure his patient prays to something he has made, "not to the Person who has made him." Wormwood may even encourage his patient to embellish the object he has made. However, if the patient ever realizes his error and consciously "directs his prayers 'not to what I think thou art but to what thou knowest thyself to be,' our situation is, for the most part, desperate."[1]

Idolatry without Idols

Idolatry occurs when we elevate any finite thing into the place that belongs to God alone. The apostle Peter says pointedly, "Whatever overcomes a man, to that he is enslaved" (2 Peter 2:19, RSV).

The temptation to practice idolatry is very subtle and can plague any of us if caught off guard. Idolatry vandalizes prayer and worship. Whether in the seventh century BC or the twenty-first century AD, objects of worship always fail. The Holy Spirit works faithfully to expose this very serious sin.

One reason the prophets find it difficult to get the people to confront their idolatrous practices is that they try to mix worship of God with worship of idols. For instance, when naming their children, parents often give names borrowed from both the worship of God and the worship of Baal. In the Jerusalem temple, King Manasseh (r. 687–643 BC) overtly combines worship of God with worship of pagan deities. He places altars to them in the temple, burns his son as an offering to the host of heaven, and persecutes those who try to be singularly obedient to God (2 Kings 21:1–26; see also Jer. 7:27–34).

Judah has no reason to forget that making covenant with God requires loving the Lord "with all your heart, and with all your soul, and with all your might" (Deut. 6:5, NRSV). They should know God will not tolerate mixing worship of God with that of pagan deities (Isa. 42:5–8). The prophets warn that prayers offered in an environment of unfaithfulness will fail and that the gods the people mix with the worship of God will come to grief. God does not share his glory with idols. But the people refuse to obey (Jer. 2:4–13). They exchange the glory of God for something unprofitable (v. 11).

The prophets' warnings remain true today. We must be willing to admit instances where we have tried to mix worship of God with worship of idols of our own making. We should regularly invite the Spirit to turn the searchlight on our values and loyalties.

Often in the church's history, the Holy Spirit has shaken everything that can be shaken so "what cannot be shaken may remain" (Heb. 12:27, RSV). In the sixteenth century, the Spirit shook the church so it could rediscover that we are reconciled to God, by grace, through faith alone.

With the Spirit's guidance, let's dig around a little in our lives and prayers. We may uncover gods we might have tried to combine with worship of the true God. Let the Holy Spirit do some shaking. He might find some scarecrows in our cucumber fields. Let's consider six gods.

The god of Self-Interest

Our age is often described as narcissistic (an inordinate self-love that can't distinguish between the self and external objects). Narcissism is idolatrous. It eventually destroys its host, just as it does Narcissus in the ancient Greek myth.

Prayer that places our interests at the center of the universe generates a god that needs to fail. God is certainly concerned about each of us and our needs. But a Christian's first and controlling interest should be to advance the kingdom of God, including loving our neighbors as ourselves. Christian prayer begins and ends in worship and adoration. The Lord's Prayer begins with "Holy is your name. Your will be done. Your kingdom come." Only after that, and in that spirit, may we then say, "Give us this day . . ."

The narcissistic distortion of prayer obstructs worship, community, and mission. It reduces other people to secondary roles, even making them tools for achieving selfish interests.

By contrast, when Jesus summarizes the Law, he says, "'You shall love the Lord your God with all your heart, and with all your soul, and with all your mind.' This is the greatest and first commandment. And a second is like it: 'You shall love your neighbor as yourself'" (Matt. 22:37–39, NRSV).

We don't need to go far to hear the god of narcissism being petitioned. The largest church in America is built upon self-interest.[2] Our pagan culture of immediate gratification primes the pump through advertising and social media.

Eventually this god will fail. To be truly Christian and received by the living God, the Holy Spirit must expose and expel the narcissist god, wherever it lurks.

The god of Happiness

We are bombarded by advertising crafted to convince us that the chief end of life is happiness and comfort. Our culture craves happiness and exploits all options for obtaining it. One popular book tells Christians how they can be happy seven days a week.[3] Unless we are diligent, aspirations that deify happiness and send us endlessly chasing it can worm their way into our primary understanding of Christian discipleship.

Happiness relies heavily on *favorable* circumstances. Remove those, and happiness vaporizes. The advertising industry taps an endless stream of material options to keep favorable circumstance well supplied.

Too many Christians have been deceived into believing that achieving happiness is a primary Christian virtue. In fact, the New Testament never mentions happiness as essential for Christian discipleship. The apostles never pray for happiness in their letters. If happiness were a primary Christian goal, Jesus would not go to the cross; Stephen would avert being stoned to death; Paul would not spend so much time in Roman jails; and Peter would not be crucified upside down in Rome.

So, if happiness is not a principal Christian virtue, what replaces it? Joy in the Holy Spirit (Acts 13:52). Jesus prays that his *joy* remain with his disciples (John 15:11; 17:13). "Unutterable and exalted joy," the apostle Peter says, belongs to those who "have been born anew to a living hope through the resurrection of Jesus Christ" (1 Peter 1:3, 8, RSV). Peter writes this to a church undergoing persecution. Paul prays for the Roman Christians, "May the God of hope fill you with all joy and peace in believing, so that you may abound in hope by the power of the Holy Spirit" (Rom. 15:13, NRSV). Unlike happiness, Christian joy doesn't vaporize when circumstances change (Rom. 14:17; 15:13; 2 Cor. 7:4; 8:2; Gal. 5:22).

This central theme of Christian joy repeatedly appears in the Gospels and Epistles (John 16:24; 17:13; Rom. 15:13; 1 Peter 1:8). The resurrection of Jesus Christ and the gift of the Holy Spirit are the sources and guarantee of joy. It rests upon the certainty of Christian hope and is accompanied by the peace of God. The apostle Paul says the essence of God's kingdom "is not food and drink," upon which happiness depends, "but righteousness and peace and joy in the Holy Spirit" (Rom. 14:17, NRSV).

Jails, shipwrecks, violent mobs, and the Jewish and Roman authorities all give Paul ample opportunity to prove he believes this. He tells the Philippian Christians about his joy in the Lord: "I have learned to be content with whatever I have. I know what it is to have little, and I know what it is to have plenty. . . . I can do all things through him who strengthens me" (Phil. 4:11–13, NRSV).

Let's admit it: Most of us want to be happy, and most of us enjoy being around happy people. We enjoy basic comforts and try to attain them. But being happy is not the same as turning it into a god that we confuse with the God who graces us with "joy and peace . . . by the power of the Holy Spirit" (Rom. 15:13).

The god of happiness will not be easily banished, for it is the currency of our social universe. It entices many Christians. The god of happiness is one of the powers against which we wrestle (Eph. 6:12). It must be "crucified with Christ" (Gal. 2:20).

Henri Nouwen points us to Jesus for instruction. "In our world, joy . . . means the absence of sorrow and sorrow the absence of joy. But such distinctions do not exist in God. Jesus, the Son of God, is the man of sorrows, but also the man of complete joy." Jesus has called his disciples to share in that joy. Those who have come to know Christ's joy do not deny the sorrow and darkness in the world, "but they choose not to live in it. They . . . celebrate the gifts they have received and live in constant anticipation of the full anticipation of God's glory."[4]

The god of Material Blessing

The third god is the pervasive notion that material and physical blessings are principal evidences of God's presence and approval, and a prize benefit of faith. This god can take on grotesque forms. Or it can subtly creep into the church unrecognized. It is present among us when we evaluate people and give them positions based on what they own or on their status in society. Notice its footprints where numerical growth is equated with increase in the kingdom of God. It resides among us when physical and material well-being monopolize our prayers.

James deals forcefully with this idol: "My brothers and sisters, do you with your acts of favoritism really believe in our glorious Lord Jesus Christ? . . . Has not God chosen the poor in the world to be rich in faith and to be heirs of the kingdom that he has promised to those who love him?" (James 2:1, 5, NRSV).

Jesus leaves no doubt about materialism. Beginning with the Beatitudes in the Sermon on the Mount, and extending all the way to the suffering Servant on the cross, he judges the god called materialism as a child of hell and a sworn enemy of the cross. If the One beside whom there is none other is to be the center of our worship, the goal of our prayers, and the governor of our lives, then the god named *materialism* must be sent back to the forest, where it belongs (Isa. 44:14), rather than be allowed to enter the temple of the Lord (Rom. 12:1–2; 1 Cor. 6:19–20).

The god of Faith Void of Justice

The fourth god the Holy Spirit works to expose is the notion that we can love God without doing justice and showing loving-kindness to our neighbors. The belief that salvation is a private contract that can be signed, sealed, and delivered apart from our neighbors is rampant in popular Christianity. Hell would like nothing more than a salvation that doesn't include neighbors, that doesn't confront racism, class consciousness, gender prejudice, illiteracy, and economic exploitation of the vulnerable.

Prophets Amos and Micah blast all forms of religion that encourage people to make under-the-table deals with God, sidestepping mercy and justice. *Forget it,* Amos says, *all such deals are bogus.* Speaking through Amos, God says, "Take away from me the noise of your songs." In their place, "Let justice roll down like waters, and righteousness like an ever-flowing stream" (Amos 5:23–24, RSV).

Through Jeremiah, God asks the people of Judah, *Is not this to know me—to do justice and righteousness and to judge the cause of the poor and needy?* (see Jer. 22:15–17, RSV).

Those who will inherit the kingdom when Christ comes in his glory will be those to whom he can say, "I was hungry and you gave me food, I was thirsty and you gave me something to drink, I was a stranger and you welcomed me, I was naked and you gave me clothing, I was sick and you took care of me, I was in prison and you visited me" (Matt. 25:35–36, NRSV).

The god of Village Deities

The fifth god is actually a cluster: village deities. When people ask, "How many Hindu gods are there?" the answer is often, "How many villages are in India?" Can village deities proliferate among Christians? If we query some of our prayers, the answer is yes. Village deities limit the range of God's interest and power to our own physical needs, family, nation, denomination, race, and/or social class.

The prophet Jonah tries to reduce Yahweh to a village deity. He wants God's love and willingness to forgive to be restricted only to the Jews. Jonah becomes angry because God will not comply. God is willing to forgive the wicked Ninevites just as he forgave Jonah's rebellious kinsmen.

One or more village deities hold sway over many Pharisees who confront Jesus. They bitterly reject Jesus because he violates the rigid boundaries they have erected. They want nothing to do with the kind of God Jesus proclaims (Matt. 9:10–13; Luke 5:30; 13:10–17; John 4:1–42).

We should know better, but sometimes when we pray, God seems to be no bigger than half a log made into an idol of the kind Isaiah ridicules (Isa. 44:9–20). He certainly doesn't look like the Creator and sustainer of the universe, the holy One, the Lord of all in whom "all things hold together" (Col. 1:17). He doesn't sound like the Father who "sends rain on the just and the unjust" (Matt. 5:45, RSV).

The Holy Spirit works diligently to set us free from our village deities.

The god of Proof

The sixth god is the pagan practice of putting God to the test, which means trying to decide the conditions under which God can prove he is God. The tempter has no ploy more deceptive and ruinous of prayer and discipleship than this one. He tries to convince God's people that setting conditions is an expression of faith when, in fact, it is just the opposite. This god plagues much of popular Christianity.

Satan uses this tactic to tempt Jesus. In so many words, he says, *Let's see whether you really are the Son of God. Jump off the pinnacle of the temple. If God sends angels to catch you, then we'll know.* The tempter wants Jesus to call the shots, to decide the terms by which the Father can prove himself.

Throughout Jesus's earthly ministry some try to set the conditions for following Jesus. *Hey, Jesus; we don't yet believe. But we'll give you another chance to convince us. Perform one more miracle, one more sign; then we will get on board* (see Luke 23:32–35; John 6:25–34). Jesus never falls for that trap. He knows that performing for these people on command will never lead to their radical trust in God or to loving discipleship. Testing God is simply a matter of putting God on a short leash, for immediate control.

The god of proof springs straight from Satan, the father of all lies. It is this spirit of unbelief that emptied heaven of the devil and his allies, and Adam and Eve from the garden of Eden.

In Gethsemane and on the cross, Jesus rebukes Satan's village deity that tests God. "My Father, if it is possible, let this cup pass from me; yet not what I want but what you want" (Matt. 26:39, NRSV).

Do not confuse the warning against testing with legitimately placing our petitions before God. The Father urges his children to present their petitions to him. But we must do so in trust and worship. We wait to see how God will implement his will.

Conclusion

Now is a good time to return to the prophet Habakkuk. When we left him in chapter 1, he was despondent. God was a disappointment, and Habakkuk wanted everyone to know it.

In the second chapter of Habakkuk, God tells the prophet that those who live as God's friends will live by faith. They will not place their trust in idols, kings, and armies. They will not assess God's faithfulness by every contrary wind that blows. Their trust will be anchored in God's character and in his long record of faithfulness to himself and to his people (Hab. 2:4).

Well, the message gets through. Finished with testing and judging God, in chapter 3 Habakkuk worships God as God, in radical trust, with no strings attached.

> Though the fig tree does not blossom,
>   and no fruit is on the vines;

though the produce of the olive fails
and the fields yield no food;
though the flock is cut off from the fold
and there is no herd in the stalls,
yet I will rejoice in the LORD;
I will exult in the God of my salvation.
GOD, the Lord, is my strength.
Hab. 3:17–19

NINE
IN DEFENSE OF DOUBT

Santiago and Molly

Santiago, a professor of European history at a South American university, asks, "What if that horse had not stumbled? What if Theodosius II had not died?"

Most Christians in western Christianity believe that, though Christ was one person, he was fully human and fully divine—two natures in one person. The Council of Chalcedon declared this as orthodox doctrine in 451 AD (". . . our Lord Jesus Christ, at once complete in Godhead and complete in manhood, truly God and truly man. . .").[1]

But at that time many Christians believed Christ possessed only one nature—the divine. They believed his human nature was indistinctly folded into his divine nature. In that era the church was bitterly, even violently, divided over this point of doctrine. Mobs of monks could be called upon to intimidate supporters of each side. Flavian, a patriarch of Constantinople who supported the Two Nature position, died after being maltreated by a mob.

Emperors and empresses chose sides. What the emperor or empress at the time believed usually reigned as orthodox. Bishops were often promoted or deposed depending on whether they were doctrinally approved by the imperial court.

Theodosius II (401–450 AD) supported the One Nature position. Largely because of his support, the One Nature party carried the day, particularly in the East. But alas! In July 450, the horse Theodosius II was riding stumbled. The emperor was sent sprawling. He was badly injured and died a few days later. A military leader named Marcian succeeded him. Marcian supported the Two Nature position. This position triumphed at the Council of Chalcedon and became the orthodox doctrine for the church, though most Christians in Egypt and other places in the East rejected it.

What if Theodosius's horse had not stumbled? What if he had not died? In all likelihood, rather than becoming orthodox and establishing the theology of Roman Catholics and Protestants alike, the Two Nature party would have become a minor, persecuted portion of Christianity. And European history would likely have taken a significantly different turn.

Santiago, the professor, knows this history well. It is the poster child for his doubts.

Santiago was reared in the church and continues to attend fairly regularly. His wife, Adriana, has been a stalwart Christian since childhood. For her, faith in the Lord and belief in God's sovereign guidance of church history seem to come naturally. If she is ever plagued by doubt, it certainly doesn't show.

For Santiago, however, faith is difficult. He is aware of many "accidents" such as the stumbling horse, which, had they turned out differently, as they could have, would have redirected history, including the shape of Christianity. "How," Santiago asks, "can I place my trust in something as precarious as a stumbling horse? What would faith mean if obtaining it requires intellectual dishonesty?"

There is also Molly, an astrophysicist, who knows a thing or two about the character and future of the universe. Raised in the church, she knows the Bible and Christian doctrine well. She knows that, according to Christian teaching, God is supposed to extensively redeem the earth. In fact, according to the book of Revelation, the redeemed earth will be the site of the glorious new Jerusalem John sees coming down from heaven (Rev. 21:2–27). She knows what the book of Romans teaches regarding the earth's future: "The creation waits in eager expectation for the children of God to be revealed. . . . the creation itself will be liberated from its bondage to decay and brought into the freedom and glory of the children of God" (Rom. 8:19, 21). The majesty of these expectations attracts Molly, just as it does other Christians.

But Molly has a problem. She cannot reconcile these elegant expectations with what she knows about the future of our solar system. Our average-sized sun, upon which all life on earth depends, is among more than 100 billion stars in the Milky Way. Like all stars, it is steadily burning through its nuclear fuel. Its fuel will last another 5 billion years and then expire. In its final death throes, the sun will become a dim, cool, black dwarf. Its ability to support life on earth will expire long before then but not before the sun's expansion has vaporized the earth. Whatever the final details of the sun's demise, our solar-dependent earth is destined to perish long before the sun blinks out.

Molly tries as hard as anyone to be a cooperating believer. But expecting her, in the interest of docile church agreement, to ignore the immense distance between what she reads in Scripture and what she knows as an astrophysicist would amount to requiring intellectual suicide. Such denial by Molly would be downright immoral. Molly's life in the church is often painful, particularly when she hears Christians refuse to take her questions seriously.

What are we supposed to do with folks like Santiago and Molly, for whom intellectual honesty makes belief difficult? Is there a place in the church, in the Christian faith, for them? Should we issue an ultimatum? "Get in or get out! Remain as a believer, or exit as an unbeliever! Don't pollute our youth and young Christians! But if you choose to stay, keep your problems to yourself!"

Santiago and Molly are among many for whom faith is difficult. Because of their questions, they can easily be made to feel like troublemakers and outcasts. Should they be shunted off into silent exile? Or is there a defense for their doubt, even if they are never able to achieve the peace everyone else seems to enjoy?

Doubt in the Name of Truth

Theologians such as St. Augustine and Paul Tillich saw something many of us miss. They realized people like Santiago and Molly doubt not *against* truth, but *in the name of* truth. And, because Jesus Christ is the way, the truth, and the life (John 14:6), without realizing it, they doubt *in his name*. This answer speaks to the integrity of truth at its deepest, most profound levels. It assigns truth such ultimate seriousness that to infringe upon it through intellectual cowardice would constitute an explicitly dishonest, immoral—even sinful—act. The unease with which Santiago and Molly live emerges from their binding respect for truth, for coherence, and for the morality of commitment. They believe the Father of all truth would be dishonored by intellectual chicanery.

Honest doubt in the interest of truth is certainly closer to the kingdom of God than is superficial belief, faith reduced to strict mental assent to doctrine, or faith thought of as an opportunity to extract some blessing from God. At least Santiago and Molly recognize the comprehensive dimensions of and requirements associated with faith.

The God of grace and truth does not require a person to surrender honesty as the price for gaining divine approval. Rather, he is the patient God, who—through prevenient grace—works in varied ways to move persons toward radical faith. Jesus's ministry displays a respect for honesty and an absence of condemnation. How else are we to explain his winsome conversation with a Samaritan woman who was probably so shunned by others that she came to draw well water at an irregular time of the day (John 4:1–42)?

John Wesley distinguishes between the faith of servants who "fear the LORD, who find great delight in his commands" (Ps. 112:1), and the faith of children: "God hath sent forth the Spirit of his Son into your hearts, crying, Abba, Father" (Gal. 4:6).[2]

Wesley's distinction can be called into service here. There are persons for whom the confident and comforting faith of a child may not currently be an option. They are not cynics. They strive to live with integrity. Paradoxically, their honest doubts actually place them in the wider precincts of truth and faith.

In the name of the God of all truth, let the church embrace the Santiagos and Mollys who live among us. The church has a responsibility to take their questions seriously. They challenge us to work hard to explain the coherence and beauty of the Christian faith. They are neither obstacles to be overcome nor worrisome impediments to be sidelined.

Jesus is the one about whom Isaiah prophesies: "A bruised reed he will not break, and a smoldering wick he will not snuff out" (Matt. 12:20).

TEN
WHEN GOD HIDES

JAWS DROPPED in 2009 when some of the private writings of Mother Teresa (1910–1997) appeared, published as *Come Be My Light: The Private Writings of the Saint of Calcutta*. No twentieth-century Christian was more admired for her love for God and the earth's dispossessed. For almost fifty years, she extended inexhaustible love and care to the poor of Calcutta, India. If ever a person walked and talked with God on a regular basis, if ever anyone's prayers were faithfully heard and answered by God, it was the prayers of Mother Teresa. She had a steady cheerful demeanor and was always ready to encourage others. At least, that was the image we had of her. But when *Come Be My Light* appeared, a darker side of Teresa's walk with the Lord surfaced, surprising her admirers and shocking some of her closest friends. Much of her life was pockmarked by an inner darkness that made her feel alone and estranged from God. She knew the meaning of "the dark night of the soul," about which St. John of the Cross (1542–1591) and St. Thérèse of Lisieux (1873–1897) spoke.

In spite of a deep, even painful longing for God, many times Teresa felt unwanted, even repulsed by God. Committed to being an apostle of joy, she often teetered on the precipice of despair; for long periods she was plagued by a silent and hidden God. "Do not think that my spiritual life is strewn with roses—that is the flower which I hardly ever find on my way. Quite the contrary, I have more often as my companion 'darkness.' And when the night becomes very thick—and it seems to me as if I will wind up in hell—then I simply offer myself to Jesus."[1]

Teresa speaks for many children of God who have encountered what seems to be a silent and hidden God. It is an odyssey in which all the once-familiar markers vanish and all comforting words from God become mute. Even supportive counsel from Christian friends cannot penetrate this thick barrier. Although God is spoken to, even yelled at, God does not speak in return. Tortured by faith's dark night, the soul grasps for some limb or outcropping as the descent into silence and loneliness intensifies. Heaven turns to brass. Prayers falter like dying sparks. This was what Mother Teresa at times experienced.

The Hiddenness of God

A profound mystery in Israel's life with God, one that scholars discuss but cannot fully explain, is the silence and hiddenness of God. It is the experience of a God who, to all appearance, sometimes seems passive and unresponsive to fervent appeals voiced by his people. Isaiah states the matter plainly: "Truly, you are a God who hides [Hebrew *sathar*, to conceal] . . . O God of Israel, the Savior" (Isa. 45:15, NRSV). On occasion in the Old Testament, disobedience or moral failure is interpreted as the reason for God's hiddenness and silence (Deut. 31:16–18; 32:19–20; Ps. 89:46; Isa. 59:2; Mic. 3:4).

If disobedience and severe moral lapse were the only reason for God hiding, an explanation would be readily available and straightforward. But that is only part of the story. In other instances there is no apparent reason, and Israel's response becomes downright accusatory as though God has flat-out failed to be God, failed to keep his promise as a responsive, covenantal partner. The mood comes close to accusing God of moral failure or cowardice. Psalm 10 boldly asks, "Why, O Lord, do you stand far off? Why do you hide yourself in times of trouble?" (v. 1, NRSV; see also 13:1). Engulfed by unidentified terrors, and crying out for help without response, the psalmist questions, "Why, LORD, do you reject me and hide your face from me?" (88:14).

However, that language is mild, almost timid, when compared with Psalm 44, in which God is charged with dereliction of duty in time of crisis. Simply put, God went AWOL when the battle started, is simply nowhere to be found. Israel has boasted to the nations of God's power and faithfulness. But when the chips are down, God fails to back up the boast, abandons Israel, and leaves them to retreat before their enemies. Deserted, Israel becomes "a reproach to our neighbors" (Ps. 44:13). The harsh accusation rolls on until, finally, the psalmist accuses God of being asleep on the job. "Awake, Lord! Why do you sleep? Rouse yourself! Do not reject us forever. Why do you hide your face and forget our misery and oppression?" (44:23–24). The psalm closes without a whisper of response from God.

The most sustained display of God's silence is found in the book of Job, where, in dramatic form, the most difficult questions of faith and the lived crises of life are openly aired. Job's accusers—Eliphaz, Bildad, and Zophar—think they have God and life figured out. They are confident that the world is governed by a morally consistent, reliable God whose ways are clearly comprehensible: *People suffer because they have sinned. Examine yourself and admit your own disobedience. God's displeasure and remoteness is your own fault!*

Job is willing to admit guilt, if he is proven to be a disobedient sinner. But, until then, there is no way to reconcile his friends' orthodoxy with the wretchedness of his life. As part of Job's reply to his accusers (12:1–14:22), he tells God in so many words, *If I have sinned, don't play games with me. Out with it! Tell me what my transgressions are!* (see 13:23). Job asks the same question posed by the psalmist: "Why do you hide your face and consider me your enemy?" (13:24). With a hint of sarcasm, Job queries the Almighty: "Will you torment a windblown leaf? Will you chase after dry chaff?" (13:25). Job seems to be asking God, *While you are hiding, is this how you use your time?* (13:25–27).

It is quite possible that Israel's experience of exile in Babylon helped shape the book of Job into its final form and that the experience of exile is partly being expressed in the narrative. To the extent that this is correct, exile in a foreign land, far removed from Jerusalem, becomes a fine metaphor for describing the experience of exile for God's people who, like Isaiah, the psalmist, Job, and Mother Teresa, experience God's silence and hiding.

A Path Out of the Darkness?

Where are Christians who identify with Mother Teresa and company supposed to turn? Is there a path forward, perhaps even out of the darkness? Is there counsel that doesn't ignore the mystery of God's silence and the oppressive, even maddening pain it engenders? Is there hope that transcends the blame that Eliphaz, Bildad, and Zophar administer?

Yes, but none neatly resolves the biblical witness to God's silence and hiddenness. Experience has established an indelible record in Scripture and in the lives of God's people. Ignoring that record cheapens faith and assigns it to a Pollyanna status. A religion doesn't deserve the attention and energy of honest people if it can't tackle life raw and unrefined.

Let's examine some facets of God's hiddenness that may help lead a child of God out of the darkness.

1. The Scriptures tell it like it is and thereby gain the respect of honest people. God doesn't silence desolate voices.

2. As the New Testament makes clear, the experience of the people of God with their God is woefully incomplete apart from the rich and varied witness of the Old Testament (Luke 24:21–27; John 5:39–40, 45–47), including its torturous wrestling with a sometimes silent and hidden God. The entire Bible belongs to the church and is our map for the Christian journey. We can't understand the Old Testament apart from the New, nor the New apart from the Old (John 5:39–47).

3. Though God is made known through the Scriptures, and definitively in the incarnate Son of God, God remains the sovereign God of holy love whose ways are sometimes beyond knowledge. No one more succinctly states this concept than the inspired apostle Paul. He writes letter after letter explaining the mystery of the gospel. But after working to explain how all Israel will be saved (Rom. 11:25–32), Paul exclaims:

> Oh, the depth of the riches of the wisdom and knowledge of God!
> How unsearchable his judgments,
> and his paths beyond tracing out!
> Who has known the mind of the Lord?
> Or who has been his counselor?
> Who has ever given to God,
> that God should repay them?

For from him and through him and for him are all things. To him be the glory forever! Amen. (Rom. 11:33–36)

4. It is important that we not permit our limited perception regarding God's activity to set the limits of what God is doing. We can be confident *something* is happening when it seems *nothing* is happening. The psalmist's question "Why do you sleep?" (Ps. 44:23) is prompted only by what he can see—as torturous as it is.

Habakkuk, who accuses God of standing idly by while the wicked swallow up the righteous (Hab. 1:13), is extremely upset. After he calms down, God tells him that, far from being inactive, he is actually using the wicked Chaldeans as instruments of his larger purpose.

5. Recall Jesus's fulfilled promise of the gift of the Holy Spirit, the Advocate who is "with us forever" (John 14:16) and who will never "leave us desolate" (14:18, RSV), even though we may not be able to detect his designs. Many times the Holy Spirit works below the radar, so to speak. One of the most assuring and joyous promises in the New Testament is that the Holy Spirit knows our weaknesses and intercedes for us in the Father's presence (Rom. 8:22–27). This is true for every Christian, regardless of whether we are young or old, weak or strong, mobile or infirm, joyous or lamenting. On our behalf, the Holy Spirit is never truant.

6. The New Testament telegraphs a hiddenness of God that Christians sometimes bring upon themselves. It happens when we refuse to forgive those who have offended or wronged us. Refusal to forgive fractures the compact of grace (John 3:16; Rom. 5:8; Titus 3:3–7), and casts a vote for Satan's opposition to reconciliation and the peace of God.

The Lord's Prayer says, "Forgive us our debts, as we also have forgiven our debtors" (Matt. 6:12). The two expressions of forgiveness—God's and ours—are inseparable; exclude one, and the other slips away (Matt. 6:24–25; see also James 2:8). The Greek word for "debts" leaves no doubt about their gravity. The debtor is guilty. Debtors have failed in their (moral) duty. Nevertheless, desiring to receive God's forgiveness while retaining an attitude of unforgiveness is futile and self-deceptive (Matt. 6:14–15). God's forgiveness is the model for our forgiving others. *Being forgiven* should make *forgiving* possible.

In perfect concord with the Lord's Prayer, the apostle Paul exhorts Christians in Ephesus, "Be kind and compassionate to one another, forgiving each other, just as in Christ God forgave you. Follow God's example" (Eph. 4:32–5:1a; see also Col. 3:13).

The rationale behind the two commands is that, if God were a petulant grudge keeper, all of us would be hopeless. Instead, God seeks reconciliation in love and forgives the offender without trivializing the offense. If we want to be affiliated with this gracious God, we must be willing to act as we see him acting. Failure to do so implicitly withdraws our own request and need to be forgiven.

Jesus cannot be clearer. "Whenever you stand praying, forgive, if you have anything against anyone; so that your Father in heaven may also forgive you your trespasses" (Mark 11:25, NRSV; see also Matt. 5:23–24). Seeking God's forgiveness and having communion with God are conditioned by, predicated upon, forgiving our fellow debtors (Matt. 18:21–35).

A clear and compelling vision of Jesus on the cross can help remove this form of hiddenness.

7. Without wanting to sound like Eliphaz, Bildad, and Zophar, there is a final factor that needs to be added. Our own physical, emotional, psychological, and domestic states of health can have a powerful influence on our ability to hear God when God is trying to address us. When things are turbulent in our lives it is tempting, sometimes almost compelling, to think the turbulence occurs because of spiritual failures.

Years ago I suffered with a dear clergy friend gripped for two years by major depressive disorder. Held fast by feelings of sadness and emptiness, gripped by feelings of worthlessness and guilt, he mourned God's silence, absence, and hiddenness. Clinical depression, a malady that ran in his family, was the source of his darkness. What he needed most, and received, was excellent medical care. Today, he is psychologically healthy and understands the medical causes of his dark night of the soul.

If you or a friend or relative show signs of major depressive disorder, seek the prayer support of fellow Christians, certainly. But do not neglect to seek care from competent professionals who know how to help patients move toward emotional and mental health.

ELEVEN
PRAYER THAT WORDS CANNOT EXPRESS

Margaret

On the day before Margaret learned that her husband, Jeff, had multiple sclerosis, they uncovered a dark secret. They could never understand why their twenty-six-year-old son had never been able to achieve stability. He wandered from one job to the next, one friend to the next, and one place of residence to the next. Damon was bright and friendly. He made friends easily but could not focus his energies and talents productively. He struggled through college before finally graduating and had been unsuccessfully employed by three firms.

Finally, Damon asked to meet with his parents. At first he found it almost impossible to speak. Then, for three hours, he told Margaret and Jeff about a record of terrors produced by repeated childhood sexual abuse at the hands of a relative who had often served as Damon's babysitter.

Now Margaret suffers the deep anguish of Damon's fathomless pain, mistrust, and confusion. She has also been staggered by Jeff's diagnosis of rapidly advancing multiple sclerosis.

Margaret has always been a quiet but strong Christian. Prayer has been a major source of her strength and growth. No more. Two years have passed since her son's revelation and her husband's diagnosis. Damon struggles in counseling, and Jeff is becoming immobile. Margaret is beaten. She knows all the words about victorious living. She has read books about how to pray. She has listened to the sermons. But she is emotionally, physically, and religiously exhausted. She and Jeff still manage to attend church somehow. But she sometimes wonders if she would do just as well to send a mannequin in her place.

Though she has tried repeatedly, Margaret simply cannot pray. Her words fall into senseless jumbles. As far as Margaret is concerned, God has gone into full eclipse. She can only groan from someplace too deep to explore.

Maybe someday things will change for the better. Maybe Damon will emerge from counseling and become a stable son. Perhaps, like Job, some years will be given to Jeff. But presently, Margaret lives in a spiritual wasteland, void of vibrant prayer and fellowship with God.

The God Who Prays for Us

Can suffering be so religiously and psychologically immobilizing that effective prayer moves out of reach for some Christians? Can it seem horribly the case that God has inattentively drifted away? Yes. But is that painful perception correct? Do life's maulings place Christians beyond the pale of God's active and redemptive care? If this were so, we would have to admit God had met his match.

But it is not true. In the epistle to the Romans, the apostle Paul pens astonishing words that express the heavenly Father's care for Margaret and all his forlorn children. Paul's language would make little sense apart from Jesus's promises regarding the Holy Spirit (John 14:15–31; 16:5–15).

In Romans 8 Paul explains what it means to live in the power of the Holy Spirit. He tells how the Holy Spirit gives victorious life to Christians, explains what it means to be led by the Spirit, and exults in good news that Christians are God's children and joint heirs with Christ (8:1–17). Then abruptly, he begins to speak of things that "groan" (Rom. 8:18–27). This may seem like a radical shift in mood and subject. But in fact it's all part of Christian hope. Paul's language plumbs the depths of the heart of God and enfolds Margaret in inexhaustible grace.

Paul speaks of the "sufferings of this present time" (Rom. 8:18, NRSV). Suffering is not an abstract, academic topic for Paul. In service to Christ, he has endured beatings from angry mobs. Five times he has received thirty-nine lashes administered by Jewish opponents. Three times he's been beaten with rods. He has faced "beasts" in Ephesus, has been ridiculed by some of his converts, stoned, imprisoned, shipwrecked three times, and threatened by robbers (Acts 9:24; 1 Cor. 15:30–32, RSV; 2 Cor. 4:8–12; 11:16–33; Phil. 1:12–26). These all occur before Paul leaves for Rome as a prisoner of the emperor (Acts 27:1–2). Still, without loss of faith, he tells Timothy that God gives us a spirit not "of fear; but of power, and of love, and of a sound mind" (2 Tim. 1:7, KJV).

The word *groaning* is used three different times by Paul to highlight three different but closely related sufferings.

First, he speaks figuratively of all creation, the natural order (*ktisis,* an original formation, fabrication) groaning and travailing together (Rom. 8:22). The Greek word for "groan" means to moan jointly or groan together. Creation also travails. The Greek word means to have pangs *in company with*, to travail in pains *together*, and to sympathize in expectation of relief from suffering. As the second term makes clear, nature's groaning has nothing to do with despair but everything to do with hope and expectation. Paul is articulating a profound, often overlooked truth that the material world is included in the glorious inheritance that comes through Christ. In language that overwhelms our senses, the book of Revelation portrays the fulfilled inheritance (Rev. 21:1–22:5). Because people and powers currently employ nature for purposes contrary to God's will, creation longs to be rid of the abuse. It longs to enter the *shalom* of God that is its birthright in Christ. It eagerly waits "for the children of God to be revealed" at the coming of the Lord. The "creation will be liberated" as well (Rom. 8:19, 21).

Second, we who are Christians, who have received the "firstfruits of the Spirit, groan inwardly" (Rom. 8:23). The word used by Paul in this verse is associated with intense sighing. Here, sighing has nothing to do with quitting or giving up. Christians have already received God's down payment—the foretaste of God's promised completion of his kingdom. So, as we suffer, we sigh deeply in anticipation of complete relief, redemption—the "redemption of our bodies" (Rom. 8:23). Henri Nouwen has insightfully spoken of such grieving as a form of prayer. "I am beginning to see that much of praying is grieving."[1]

Third, the creation groans, Christians groan, and then Paul steps beyond our range of comprehension. He says the Holy Spirit of God intercedes for us with "groanings which cannot be uttered" (Rom. 8:26, KJV). What jolting language. The third person of the Trinity, God himself, actually suffers, groans, and identifies with our sighs and longings. It's Scripture! The Holy Spirit groans before the Father in intercession *"according to the will of God"* (v. 27, KJV, emphasis added).

In the gospel of John, Jesus tells us that one ministry of the Holy Spirit will be to teach Jesus's disciples what to say. Not only does the Holy Spirit sometimes teach us what to say, but according to Paul, in some instances, the Spirit also formulates our words and our thoughts when we cannot. As was true on the day of Pentecost, the promised Holy Spirit (John 14:26) is the great translator (Acts 2:1–12). The Spirit translates our sighs and prayers before the Father. When God's children are so distressed they can't voice a coherent word, prayer is still happening! Praise be to God.

Why would the Holy Spirit groan "with sighs too deep for words" (Rom. 8:26, NRSV)? Is God so attentive, so present, that in the depths of his own being, he sighs as one who suffers with us?

That's precisely what Paul means. The truth is too high for our comprehension (Rom. 11:33–35), but not for our waiting and longing hearts. Paul tells us that "the Spirit searches all things, even the deep things of God" (1 Cor. 2:10). When the Spirit groans in sighs too deep for words, he is revealing the depths of the heavenly Father's heart, bringing the Father's hidden pain to expression. Absolutely astonishing: The God who created the heavens and the earth suffers, groans, absorbs, carries, and accepts for himself the depths of all human suffering. Whoever heard of such a thing? The prophets Isaiah (Isa. 53:1–12) and Hosea (Hos. 2:14–23) have.

At times, God's children—the Margarets and others—are tempted to think that God, in lofty splendor, doesn't hear, is impassive, or is too busy doing bigger things. The Romans text makes clear that "groaning" isn't something God does infrequently. It happens whenever and wherever God's people suffer, when inarticulate groans escape flayed hearts and parched lips.

Be assured that all groaning and all hope are made possible by the sufferings of our Redeemer (1 Tim. 2:5; Heb. 4:14–5:10). "It was fitting that God, for whom and through whom all things exist, in bringing many children to glory, should make the pioneer of their salvation perfect through sufferings" (Heb. 2:10, NRSV).

Margaret, good news! The eternal, triune God has inextricably joined himself to his people. "O the depth of the riches and wisdom and knowledge of God!" (Rom. 11:33, RSV).

Amen!

TWELVE
PRAYER AT THE END OF LIFE

IVAN ILYICH is dying, possibly of pancreatic cancer. Five physicians with attitudes from arrogant to dishonest have offered little assistance or compassion. His family has lost patience and tends to blame him for his illness. It intrudes on their normal social life. Gerasim, the family's peasant servant, is responsible for assisting Ivan. Gerasim is the only one who offers compassion and humane care for Ivan.

In *The Death of Ivan Ilyich*,[1] Leo Tolstoy powerfully shows how the imminence of death can force one to confront his or her own history, vulnerability, and mortality. As Ivan's condition worsens, he stops looking for ways to avoid the certainty of his death. He struggles to confront his selfishness and desperate efforts to live. Ivan's wife and daughter mirror his selfishness and the way he lived before his illness. Like the rich man about whom Jesus speaks, they spend their days tearing down barns and building bigger ones (Luke 16:19–31).

Religious in only the most incidental sense possible, Ivan, at his wife's encouragement, turns to a priest and receives the sacrament of the Lord's Supper. He'll try anything.

Finally, exhausted, Ivan is in a position to hear from God. This never occurred during his life as a judge in the Russian justice system.

In a strikingly sober interchange between God and Ivan, God asks, "What do you want?"

Ivan answers, "I want to live."

God responds, "And what does it mean to live?"

Ivan cannot give a good answer.

Ivan Ilyich wants to live. But his life has been void of depth, love, community, real friendship, faith, and moral substance. *Life* has meant parties by which to impress people, card games, professional appointments, better furniture and clothes, and advantageous social contacts. At the close, he admits to himself that he never truly lived.

The irony of the story is that the *death* of Ivan Ilyich opens the door for him to live. In the closing days and hours, Ivan falls into death to his old self. "He fell through the hole and there at the bottom was a light." When Ivan "caught sight of the light . . . it was revealed to him that though his life had not been what it should have been, this could still be rectified."

Then "something rattled in his throat, his emaciated body twitched, then the gasping and rattle became less and less frequent.

"'It is finished!' said someone near him.

"He heard these words and repeated them in his soul.

"'Death is finished,' he said to himself. 'It is no more!'

"He drew in a breath, stopped in the midst of a sigh, stretched out, and died."[2]

In the riveting story of Ivan Ilyich, Tolstoy retells the New Testament truth that not until one dies can one begin to live (Matt.

16:24; Rom. 6:1–4). Tolstoy profiles a world that thinks it is alive through things, when in fact it is dead in spirit. Like Ivan, when God asks what it means to live, there is no good answer.

Do Christians have a better answer than Ivan's when they face their own deaths or the death of a loved one? Is there a distinctly Christian way to live and die? Should how we pray as we live and as we face death reveal the essence of our faith?

The Christian Desire to Live

One problem in early Christianity is that some Christians seek martyrdom by unnecessarily goading Roman authorities. Martyrs are held in high regard in the church. It is the ultimate crown. Some church leaders warn against this impulse as misrepresenting the Christian understanding of life and death.[3]

It is normal for Christians to want to live instead of die. In fact, the apostle Paul identifies death as an enemy (1 Cor. 15:26). If we were to encounter a Christian in everyday life begging for an opportunity to die, we would quickly label that person morbid, or abnormal. On the other hand, there is a proper tension between a love for life and a desire to be with the Lord. This tension is reflected in the apostle Paul's words to the church in Philippi: "For to me, to live is Christ and to die is gain. . . . I am torn between the two: I desire to depart and be with Christ, which is better by far; but it is more necessary for you that I remain in the body" (Phil. 1:21, 23–24).

The tension becomes most pointed when Christians are facing terminal illness for themselves or loved ones. If life after death with Christ is so desirable, why bombard heaven with appeals to remain on planet Earth? If heaven is such a friend, why is death such an enemy?

What Christians Believe about Life in the World

First, Christians believe human life is God's gift. It is good and should be treasured.

The Bible leaves no doubt about life's origin (Gen. 1:1–3; John 1:1–5). The creation came into existence solely through God's good action, not through inferior or nefarious powers.

"Thus says God, the LORD, who created the heavens and stretched them out, who spread out the earth and what comes from it, who gives breath to the people upon it and spirit to those who walk in it: I am the LORD" (Isa. 42:5–6a, NRSV). The New Testament names the Son of God as the One through whom all things were created (John 1:1–5; Col. 1:15–16), by whom the world is sustained (Col. 1:17), and through whom God is reconciling all things to himself (Eph. 1:15–23; Col. 1:19–20). Clearly, life is good by virtue of its origin and its goal (1 Tim. 4:4–5).

This confidence entails a solemn warning. The importance of physical existence derives from the spiritual, not vice versa, as in modern materialism, where the material is primary and the spiritual is a troublesome and unnecessary appendage of the physical. If a Christian thinks and behaves this way, then that person casts a vote for atheism.

One thing about the Bible that strikes a reader is its earthiness. It assumes this earth is a fit place for life to flourish and for knowing God. God intends for us to explore what it means to be created in his image, to rejoice in him as Creator, and to walk obediently before him. Though sin and evil plague the world, nowhere does the Bible say it results from a divine blunder. The creation announces God as its Author. "The heavens declare the glory of God; the skies proclaim the work of his hands. Day after day they pour forth speech; night after night they reveal knowledge" (Ps. 19:1–2; see also Ps. 148).

The Bible celebrates all dimensions of life. Its interests include diverse occupations, domestic life, music, merriment, and dance. Romance and marriage, urban and rural life, friendship and conflicts, successes and failures, and how to live justly and peacefully in community are there. A wealth of instruction in worship, prayer, and faith add to life's riches. Lauded saints and condemned rogues, great and small, wise and foolish, rich and poor, noble and scandalous help paint the Bible's mural of life.

A distinct, even unique, feature of how the Old Testament understands "person" can amplify our appreciation for the Bible's affirmation of life. Unlike the Greek philosopher Plato, for instance, the Hebrews think of "person" in holistic, integrated terms—including neighbor and natural environment. They do not think of people as divided into segregated compartments such as body, soul, or spirit, with some parts being more important than others. Old Testament scholar Timothy Green explains God's command to his covenant people to love him with all their heart, soul, and might (Deut. 6:4–5). Green says "heart" (*leb*) means our will, our mind—the centerpiece of our daily decision-making process. "Soul" (*nephesh*) means life force, life energy, or pulse—what we feel when we take our pulse. "Might" (Hebrew, *meod*) means everything, as in, *Love God with your everything*.[4] The whole person is God's creation and the object of God's care. The whole, integrated person engages in worship (see Rom. 12:1–2; 1 Tim. 4:1–5).

Life and the world are God's gifts, not impediments that must be avoided or overcome. God is at home in creation. In fact, God regularly gets all mixed up in the affairs of nations, families, individuals, and nature's activity. Otherwise, the incarnation of our Lord would have been impossible (John 1:1–5, 14–18; Phil. 2:5–11). The psalmist declares, "May the glory of the LORD endure forever; may the LORD rejoice in his works" (Ps. 104:31, NRSV).

Second, the Bible tells us that nothing God created, including life, should ever be given the importance that belongs to God alone, or that God never intended for it. We can celebrate, flourish, and care for God's creation, but we must never worship it. Otherwise, life will become imbalanced, grotesque, and opposed to what God intended.

For example, when physical health and survival are treated as ultimately important, permitted to run roughshod over other values, then health becomes idolatrous, a rogue in God's order. Today, the idolatry of health is fueled by an unending stream of advertisement laden with grand promises that exaggerate expectations. In a pagan environment where this idol thrives, Christians must be alert and discerning.

The Bible records instances of nations and individuals who treat nature as a deity. It details the disruptive and destructive consequences (Rom. 1:18–32). Astonished, the prophets ask, *Why would people, whom God created, fall down and worship things God created? Why worship idols instead of God?* Screwtape, the old demon assigned to instruct his nephew, Wormwood, has an answer. Humans "tend to regard death as the prime evil and survival as the greatest good . . . because we have taught them to do so."[5]

Idols change from culture to culture and from age to age. However, they never go away. In our era, technology—including medical technology—has become an idol for many. In its proper place, technology can be creatively used to enhance human life and to glorify God. But if we permit it to slip its moral harness, it can become an idol. Its value must be conditioned by a larger community of individual, familial, and social values. The overuse and misuse of health-care services in the United States is a national scandal. "Experts estimate that perhaps one-third of all U.S. health-care spending produces no benefit to the patient—and some of it actually results in harm. . . . The intensity of end-of-life care, open heart surgery, and angioplasty may cost the health care system approximately $600 billion per year in avoidable costs."[6]

Grasping for costly medical technology in a frenzied attempt to retain physical life, when prospects for meaningful life have seriously eroded, betray Christian hope for the resurrection. Resurrection people must strive to bear good witness to life eternal during and at the conclusion of physical life.

Christian Prayer at the End of Life

What we believe about God's relationship to creation has direct bearing on how we live, pray, and die. Christians should do all this in ways that derive directly from our faith. In a world where pagan values increasingly press hard against us, this need becomes more urgent but also more difficult.

Without ignoring grief and tragedy, Christians should live as robust witnesses to God the Creator. Life should be creative, celebratory, merciful, and hopeful.

But how we die should be as much a witness to Christ and the new creation as how we live. We should die as persons who know death will not terminate the work of the Creator-Redeemer, will not end our relationship with him, and will not terminate human meaning. Christians live and die in the hope of the resurrection (Titus 3:3–7). They oppose death as an enemy of the Lord but also as an enemy already defeated (1 Cor. 15:35–58; 2 Tim. 1:8–10; 1 Peter 1:13; Rev. 1:4–8, 17–18).

But what does resurrection really mean? Roman Catholic theologian Romano Guardini answers succinctly: "Resurrection consists of the transformation of the totality of our being, spirit and flesh, by the recreative power of God's love."[7] Every guarantee of such a salvation rests upon Easter, Christ's coming forth from the grave by the power of the Spirit in his transfigured humanity, "the first-born of all creation" (Col. 1:15, RSV), "the first-born from the dead" (Col. 1:18, RSV), our eternal pathfinder (Heb. 2:10).

Two Subversive Errors to Avoid

At least two fundamental Christian beliefs should distinguish Christians when facing death.

The *first* belief stands in sharp contrast to something Greek philosopher Socrates (c. 470–399 BC), Plato's teacher, taught. The Athenian Senate sentenced Socrates to death by poison—specifically, he would be forced to drink tea made from hemlock. Before he died, his disciples grieved. Socrates reprimanded and instructed them, saying that their grief showed ignorance of the soul, the most meaningful and indestructible part of humans. By contrast, the body is transitory. With its emotions, hungers, and weaknesses, it is just a momentary, animated shell, while the soul is real and permanent.[8] We will be much better off, Socrates said, when the soul is released from the body at death. People who think of death as an enemy place too much emphasis on "bodily pleasures and adornments."[9]

Those who have lived a life of "surpassing holiness," Socrates insisted, don't see death as an enemy. They know that when they die their souls will live "altogether without bodies, and reach habitations even more beautiful, which is not easy to portray."[10]

When the time came for Socrates to drain the cup of hemlock, he "received it quite cheerfully."[11]

At no point has Christian doctrine been more grievously subverted than in a popular substitution of Socrates (and Plato) for what the New Testament teaches. For many, Socrates's belief regarding an eternal soul and a permanently perishing body has replaced the New Testament promise and hope of bodily resurrection. It is common to hear Christians speak of having eternal souls that cleanly survive physical death and sail on to heaven. They say the soul is really the important and lasting part of the person. The corpse is just dispensable rubbish. Because the soul is permanent and important, the material, mental, social, and emotional dimensions of life permanently expire without loss. Socrates and Plato would applaud such a belief.

Here lurks a subtle idolatry that can snare well-meaning Christians. Trust is placed in the idea of an eternal soul rather than in the risen Christ, who alone is our hope. Apart from Christ, who is our resurrection and life (John 11:25), we have no hope at all (1 Cor. 15:19). Substituting an eternal soul for the Christian hope of resurrection voids and redefines the gospel of Jesus Christ, turning it into a narrowly interested, otherworldly philosophy. It is far removed from hope for the resurrection of the body, hope for the salvation of the whole person as preached by Jesus (John 5:25–29; 6:35–40; 11:25–26) and the apostles.

If Socrates and Plato are correct, then Easter is an error-plagued myth (1 Cor. 15:12–22). There would have been no need for Jesus's bodily resurrection. His eternal soul would have escaped his mutilated body and peacefully ascended to the Father, unaffected by the blood and gore of Calvary. His worthless body would have rotted in the borrowed tomb! That is the price and implication if we insert Socrates into Christian doctrine.

The apostle Paul permits no such error. He is absolutely clear that if we abandon the hope of the resurrection of the body, then the entire Christian faith collapses (1 Cor. 15:29–58; Phil. 3:20–21). There is an uncompromising reason for this. If God is the Creator of the body, as we believe, then to abandon any part of the person to hopeless corruption guarantees that the work of the Creator on the cross of Calvary failed. Part of what was affected by the fall would remain unredeemed. Death, and its accompanying chaos that entered through Adam, would have the final word (Rom. 5:18–19; 1 Cor. 15:21–23). And humankind would still need a redeemer.

But the Father did raise Jesus from the grave, just as Christ promises to "raise up at the last day" all those who "eat the flesh of Son of Man and drink his blood" (John 6:39–40, 44, 53–58, NRSV), an invitation that would have repulsed Socrates. Christ is the "firstfruits" of our promised resurrection. "For as in Adam all die, so in Christ all will be made alive. But each in his own turn: Christ the firstfruits; then, when he comes, those who belong to him" (1 Cor. 15:22–23).

Paul was grounded in the doctrine of creation and the fall. Socrates was not; he would have been scandalized to think that a good God would actively create, much less become associated with, a material world. By contrast, the apostle Paul has encountered the victorious, risen, and ascended Christ (Acts 9:1–6; 1 Cor. 15:1–8) being preached by confident Christians.

Paul knows that partial redemption is no redemption at all. The whole created person is the subject of salvation (Phil. 3:20–21). Short of that, there is no gospel. We are "still in our sins," our "faith is futile," and Paul is a "false witness" (1 Cor. 15:12–19).

The *second* subversive belief that can affect Christians thrives in a secularist social climate. It is the belief that physical life is all there is. Unlike Socrates, many in our culture believe that when people die, everything about them completely and permanently perishes. Their best hope is that they will have made a contribution to others and will be remembered well. Otherwise, when one dies, meaning as a person permanently ceases.

This belief can motivate persons to hold on to physical life at all costs. Squeeze from life all you can, and expend all resources required to do so, for afterward, there is nothing more.

The apostle Paul says such people think, "Let us eat and drink, for tomorrow we die" (1 Cor. 15:32). The contemporary version of this philosophy is "You go around only once, so grab all the gusto you can."

Sadly, when facing death, many Christians sound more like frightened pagans than confident, hope-filled Christians. They try to bargain with God. In panic, they act and pray as though physical life is the supreme value. Functionally, they act as though hope extends no further than what health and medical technology can provide (1 Cor. 15:19). For these Christians, desperation, rather than trust and the peace of God, fuels prayer.

Contrast these two errors with the good news delivered to the Corinthian Christians:

For this perishable body must put on imperishability, and this mortal body must put on immortality. When this perishable body puts on imperishability, and this mortal body puts on immortality, then the saying that is written will be fulfilled:

"Death has been swallowed up in victory."

"Where, O death, is your victory? Where, O death, is your sting?"

The sting of death is sin, and the power of sin is the law. But thanks be to God, who gives us the victory through our Lord Jesus Christ. (1 Cor. 15:53–57, NRSV)

Socrates thought the holy person should think of death as a friend. But Paul saw death as an enemy, the final enemy. "The last enemy to be destroyed is death" (1 Cor. 15:26, NRSV). This enemy that tried to separate the Son from the Father and that threatens to separate God from his redeemed people was destroyed on the cross and announced on Easter morning. Its fate has been sealed. In that certainty, we wait for the hope of the resurrection (1 Peter 1:3).

Questions about Prayers at the End of Life

1. What should Christians request when they pray for those who are dying?

Understandably, most of us are uncertain about how we should pray for the terminally ill. We desire to be helpful and to communicate our sorrow. We want God to do all his will permits. At the same time, we recognize medical diagnoses that point to imminent death. So how are we to pray?

First, we pray that the peace of the resurrected Christ will enfold the person. To pray for the peace of Christ is to pray that the person will be assured that nothing, death included, will be able to separate him or her from the love of God in Christ Jesus our Lord (Rom. 8:38–39). Even if the person is unconscious, it is appropriate to pray for the peace of Christ.

Second, we can pray for physical healing. Through our intercession, God may act to restore health to a dying person. Many are such testimonies, and we should always be prepared in faith to receive the grace of physical healing. However, this is not an encouragement to bargain with God or to speak carelessly. It's a simple request, in the same vein as Jesus in Gethsemane: *If you will . . . Nevertheless, your will be done.*

At the same time, we should pray that God will help the dying person receive the grace to die. The grace to die is the gift that makes it possible to release our lives—our successes and our failures—into the care of our Redeemer. The grace to die includes confidence that because Christ lives, we will live also. If conditions make it impossible for the dying person to "rejoice in our hope of sharing the glory of God" (Rom. 5:2, RSV), then we who remain can do it for them. The grace to die assures that being in Christ is life eternal (John 17:3; see also 5:24; 6:50–71). The grace to die enfolds God's children in the Alpha and the Omega, "who is and who was and who is to come (Rev. 1:8, RSV).

2. Should Christians ever pray for another's death to occur?

As strange as it may seem, the answer is yes. With the medical community's ability to sustain physical life far beyond any hope of meaningful recovery, this question's urgency and practicality increases. In many instances, the only thing keeping a loved one alive is artificial hydration and respiration. Were it not for that, the person would be dead.

But in many instances, neither the health-care professionals nor we the family can simply disconnect life-support systems. So we wait through what may seem like a pointless eternity.

In such instances, a person who loves the dying individual can offer as a Christian prayer, "Lord, take her. Take her now into your care and keeping. Help her now to give back to you the life you gave to her." Such a prayer is not unloving. The one who prays it—perhaps a spouse, for example—may know that the prolonged illness, from which this person will likely not recover, has placed extreme strains on a family's resources. Permitting this knowledge to become a factor in how we pray is not wrong.

It may also be important to give a loved one permission to die. Sometimes loving, terminally ill people think they must hold on for the benefit of spouses or children. In such instances, pray that the Christ from whose care none of us can ever be separated will grace the room with his assurance and peace.

3. Should Christians ever stop praying for one who is dying?

Many of us have reached a point, while attending a dying relative or friend, when we ask, "Should we stop praying?" We should *never* stop praying. But we may change the focus and direction of our prayers. We may stop praying for healing and pray that God will help the person and us accept death in a truly Christian way.

Claude Thompson, a theologian and professor at Emory University in the 1960s and early 1970s, died of cancer. Mrs. Thompson reached a point at which she stopped praying for Dr. Thompson's healing and began to pray that God would bless their remaining days together. She also prayed that God would prepare both of them for Dr. Thompson's death. God heard her prayer.

On the day of Dr. Thompson's funeral at the Candler School of Theology, the congregation sang songs of Christian affirmation and hope. At the close of the service, as Mrs. Thompson left the church, everyone could see by the look on her face that the Holy Spirit was helping her draw freely upon the Christ who had promised never to leave or forsake her.

4. How should Christians pray after God fails to heal?

Perhaps we've asked God to heal a family member, a friend, or a leader, but the petition was not granted. We may have prayed for years and been confident healing would come. But it doesn't. How should we respond? On the one hand, we confess with the apostle Paul, "How unsearchable are [God's] judgments and how inscrutable his ways!" (Rom. 11:33, RSV). On the other hand, we pray for grace to say, "Praise God from whom all blessings flow," for "from him and through him and to him are all things. To him be the glory for ever. Amen" (Rom. 11:36, RSV; see also 1 Tim. 1:17).

5. How should we pray for terminally ill children?

It can be difficult enough to accept an adult's death, but perhaps watching a child suffer is even worse. We're struck by the fact that death will shatter a child's potential before he or she can explore the rich gifts God has given. Often disease will have stalked the child for months, leaving him or her but a shadow of the former self.

Pray that God will empower the parents of these precious children to place God's gift to them back in the Gift Giver's hands. Pray that God will make it possible for parents to love and worship the Lord of life in spite of a child's death.

A child's terminal illness is a time to embody the grace, compassion, and love of our Lord. It is also a time to refrain from saying foolish things about God, such as "God needed another angel in heaven." In the interest of being empathetic, well-intended people can easily indict God as a killer. A child's terminal illness is a time to speak to him or her about God's presence and love, and of how Jesus received children when he was among us. It may also be a time for parents sensitively and candidly to explain to siblings the facts about a child's illness.

When our youngest daughter was nineteen months old, she was diagnosed with spinal meningitis. When she was admitted to the hospital, the medical personnel told us that our stiff, very sick child might not live through the night. God's promise was, *My presence will be with you.* Our belief about trusting God was being tested. We humbly prayed, "God, she's yours first. We've done all we can. We're tired. Please let us sleep." We slept through the night.[12]

> The King of love my shepherd is,
> whose goodness faileth never.
> I nothing lack if I am his,
> and he is mine forever.
>
> In death's dark vale I fear no ill,
> with thee, dear Lord, beside me;
> thy rod and staff my comfort still,
> thy cross before to guide me.
>
> And so through all the length of days,
> thy goodness faileth never;

> Good Shepherd, may I sing thy praise
> within thy house forever.
> (Sir H. W. Baker, 1821–1877)

THIRTEEN
NO SUBSTITUTE JESUS

FLANNERY O'CONNOR (1925–1964) was a twentieth-century American writer who did much to expose the folly of superficial Christianity and the failure of all secularized efforts to replace God. She was a Roman Catholic layperson who lived in Milledgeville, Georgia. Socially odd, even grotesque, characters pass through her novels and short stories. Her characters show that people who seriously struggle with Jesus's radical conditions for discipleship are much closer to the kingdom than persons who think they can waltz in without breaking a sweat. O'Connor did through fiction what Dietrich Bonhoeffer, the twentieth-century German Christian, did through theology. Both insist that "the call to discipleship is the call to come and die."

In O'Connor's stories, socially ugly persons enter the kingdom while beautiful people, who believe they have the gospel under control, are left out. "All my stories," O'Connor wrote, "are about the action of grace on a character who is not very willing to [receive] it."[1]

When gods Try to Be God

O'Connor hoped she could help people become anchored in the God beyond all gods. She knew many of us at times fall victim to functionally reducing God to the size of a god. We too can create a substitute Jesus. But any substitute will eventually break down and have to be cast aside.

Each of us is tempted because we bear the marks of humanity's fall. Too easily we forget we have finite minds, perspectives, and interests. We're profoundly limited in our geographical, gender, economic, racial, national, and social locations. Sometimes we forget this and speak like the scholarly frog living at the bottom of a well. After studying his environment carefully, the frog wrote an authoritative, three-volume analysis of the ocean.

Flannery O'Connor and others have urged Christians to live and pray in ways that show they truly know the God who *is* (Ex. 3:13–15). She wanted Christians to distinguish between a gospel that yields a church without Jesus Christ and one that affirms with Peter, "Lord, to whom can we go? You have the words of eternal life" (John 6:68, NRSV).

Hazel Motes, the central figure in O'Connor's 1952 novel, *Wise Blood*, searches for a substitute Jesus. Hazel is one of the strangest characters in American literature. Determined to escape his mother's Jesus, he now preaches the beginning of a new church, "the Church of Truth Without Jesus Christ Crucified."[2]

But Hazel needs a new Jesus that's "all man, without blood to waste."[3] Enoch Emery, a socially awkward boy recently escaped from the Rodemill Boys' Bible Academy, finds a new Jesus for Hazel's church. He steals a mummy from a museum, carries it through the rain to his room, and temporarily places it in a washstand sanctuary meant to hold a chamber pot (a "slop jar," in cruder language). Rain-soaked, the mummy has begun to decompose. By the time it reaches Hazel, one side of its face has been partly mashed, an eyelid has split, and pale dust is seeping out.⁴

Hazel throws the "shriveled body" of the substitute Jesus against a wall. "The head popped and the trash inside sprayed out in a little cloud of dust."⁵

The story is immensely humorous, but it's also parabolic. That, Flannery O'Connor said, is what finally happens to every substitute Jesus. They are safe only when stored in museums, or washstands meant for chamber pots. When required to take the place of Jesus Christ, their heads pop, and the trash inside sprays out in a little cloud of dust.

As Jesus's disciples strive for righteousness and mature knowledge of God, we must be attentive to the possible intrusion of gods that rot, whether political, professional, monetary, physical, or ethnic. Praying to them need not be overt; it can happen subtly by placing godlike trust in them. Unrelenting honesty and vigilance is required to avoid this failure.

One classic contest in the Bible between God and a god occurs in Exodus. Through a burning bush that is not consumed, God arrests Moses's attention. He tells Moses to go back to Egypt and lead the children of Israel out of slavery.

Moses is no fool. He knows the children of Israel are slaves, and not ready for self-government. He also knows they can be contentious. More importantly, Moses appreciates Egyptian power. From childhood, he has been acquainted with Egyptian architectural grandeur and military might.

Moses owns a staff and has a family and some sheep. When God tells him to go tell Pharaoh to "let my people go!" we can almost hear his response: *Say what?* Moses basically asks God, "And when I arrive in Egypt, who am I to identify as my underwriter?

Who is backing me up?" That is an important question. In Egypt, Pharaoh is considered a personification of the sun god *Re*.

God answers, "Tell Pharaoh that 'I AM WHO I AM' has sent you" (Ex. 3:13–15, author's paraphrase). The Hebrew word is *YHWH*, or *Yahweh*, meaning "I AM WHO I AM." Another translation of *Yahweh* is "I will be who I will be." No matter how big and powerful the Pharaoh might be, the "I AM" fences him in. God will trump Pharaoh-*Re* every time. Through Moses, the "I AM" God will show Pharaoh that he is nothing more than a flimsy imposter.

The famous ten plagues (Ex. 7:8–11:10) are not meant to dazzle Pharaoh or us. This is not a publicity contest between magicians. The plagues show how the true Creator God places firm boundaries on even his strongest substitutes. That is what happens. Each plague places a limit on something Egypt's deity is supposed to control. Finally, God eliminates Pharaoh's firstborn son. Upon Pharaoh's death, his firstborn son is supposed to become god in his father's place.

What is true of the pharaoh is true of all god substitutes. Even the Canaanite Baal gods that supposedly control the weather and fertility prove to be imposters. Elijah sees to that. The Baal priests pray for fire, and nothing happens. But when Elijah prays, God sends a fire that consumes the sacrifice, the altar, and the water that was poured on the sacrifice (1 Kings 18).

The God Who Takes Us Deeper

Christian prayer is grounded in and directed toward God who is beyond all gods. Mature Christian prayer has no room for a substitute Jesus. As an expression of worship, Christian prayer is intent on letting God be God on his own terms. It is directed toward the One who *is* and who will never fail to be himself.

The Bible repeatedly distinguishes between the living God and all claimants to his identity. In fact, all such imposters are just parts of God's creation, clamoring for a position they can never successfully occupy. The Law and the prophets, Jesus, and the apostles expose this preposterous effort and declare its inglorious failure.

God doesn't draw upon existing things for his being. He *is* life. He *is* Spirit. He *is* power. He *is* grace. He *is* love. He *is* eternal. God's faithfulness to himself and to us *is* everlasting. God *is* the One who "became flesh and lived among us. . . . We have seen his glory, the glory as of a father's only son, full of grace and truth" (John 1:14, NRSV). "God," said Karl Barth, "is the One whose Name and cause are borne by Jesus Christ."[6]

The writer to the Hebrews says that "a sabbath rest still remains for the people of God" (Heb. 4:9, NRSV). The Sabbath rest partly involves arriving at a level of maturity where the God with whom we commune and whom we worship is truly the God beyond all rotting substitutes. At this level of faith and prayer, all God's children are meant to live.

Beyond all gods doesn't mean God is remote. God sojourns with us without ceasing to be God. If God's people are willing, he will rid them of every substitute Jesus, and equip them for abundant life.

William Cowper prayed:

> The dearest idol I have known,
> whate'er that idol be,
> help me to tear it from thy throne,
> and worship only thee.
> So shall my walk be close with God,
> calm and serene my frame;
> so purer light shall mark the road
> that leads me to the Lamb. *Amen.*
> (William Cowper, 1731–1800)

CONCLUSION

IN THIS BOOK we have walked with those who cannot pray and have aired some obstacles that hobble effective payer. Without minimizing the hurdles, we have seen how our faithful Lord walks with or carries his people, including those for whom prayer is a barrier.

Tommy Dorsey (1899–1993), born in Villa Rica, Georgia, was one of the best-known gospel musicians in America. In 1932 he penned a simple but powerful song called "Precious Lord, Take My Hand." The song became a favorite among Christians. It beautifully unites both those who can pray and those who can't in the care and keeping of him who promised never to leave or forsake us (Deut. 31:6).

Dorsey wrote the song amidst the tragic death of his wife and infant daughter in childbirth. Grief and confusion made it well-nigh impossible for Dorsey to pray. During his dark night he simply opened his heart and sang:

> Precious Lord, take my hand,
> Lead me on, let me stand.
> I am tired, I am weak, I am worn.
> Thro' the storm, thro' the night,
> Lead me on to the light.

Take my hand, precious Lord; lead me home. . . .
When the darkness appears
And the night draws near,
And the day is past and gone,
At the river I stand;
Guide my feet, hold my hand.
Take my hand, precious Lord; lead me home.[1]

NOTES

Chapter 1

1. I am following Bernhard Anderson's explanation of the Deuteronomic Reform under King Josiah, and of Habakkuk, one of the twelve minor prophets. Bernhard Anderson, *Understanding the Old Testament* (Englewood Cliffs, NY: Prentice Hall, 1975), 348–66.

2. Philip Yancey, *Disappointment with God* (New York: Harper Paperbacks, 1988), 24.

3. Marjorie Hewitt Suchocki, *God's Presence: Theological Reflections on Prayer* (St. Louis: Chalice Press, 1996), 2.

4. Mark Twain, *The War Prayer*, http://www.midwinter.com/lurk/making/warprayer.html. Last accessed 4 November 2015.

Chapter 2

1. Herman Melville, "Bartleby the Scrivener," *Literature of Western Civilization*, vol. 2, ed. Louis G. Locke, John Pendy Kirby, and M. E. Porter (New York: Ronald Press Co., 1952), 415–31.

2. The New York Court of Chancery was the court with jurisdiction over cases of equity in the state of New York from 1777 until 1847.

3. Albin Lesky, *Greek Tragedy* (New York: Barnes and Noble Books, 1978), 8.

4. Heather Ramsey, "10 Inspiring Stories of People Who Turned Tragedy into Triumph," LISTVERSE, December 23, 2014. http://listverse.com/2014/12/23/10-inspiring-stories-of-people-who-turned-tragedy-into-triumph. Last accessed 6 November 2015.

5. Frederick Buechner, *Telling the Truth: The Gospel as Tragedy, Comedy, and Fairy Tale* (New York: Harper and Row, 1977), 33–35.

6. Ibid.

7. Ibid., 35.

Chapter 3

1. Farah Stockman and Mac Daniel, "After 18 years in prison, 'It's great to be free,'" *Boston Globe*, March 16, 2001, B1, B4.

2. The Innocence Project *http://www.innocenceproject.org/cases-false-imprisonment/kenny-waters*. Last accessed 10 November 2015.

3. Lindsey Rogers, "Mail carrier rescues injured Hope Hull man trapped for 10 days," WSFA 12 News, July 28, 2015. *http://www.kctv5.com/story/29591577/mail-carrier-rescues-injured-hope-hull-man-stranded-for-10-days*. Last accessed 10 November 2015.

4. Karl Barth, *Dogmatics in Outline* (New York: Harper Torchbooks, 1958), 135.

5. "The Road Ahead," from *Thoughts in Solitude*, Thomas Merton, Copyright © 1958 by the Abbey of Our Lady of Gethsemani, Copyright renewed 1986 by the Trustees of the Thomas Merton Legacy Trust, Reprinted by permission of Farrar, Straus and Giroux, LLC.

Chapter 4

1. *Classics Devotional Bible* (Grand Rapids: Zondervan Publishing House, 1996), 208.

2. Luke T. Johnson, *The Writings of the New Testament: An Interpretation* (Philadelphia: Fortress Press, 1986), 546.

3. Martin Luther, "Preface to the Old Testament," *Luther's Works*, vol. 35, ed. E. Theodore Bachmann (Philadelphia: Muhlenberg, 1960), 235–36.

4. Sources consulted: *The Expositor's Bible Commentary* (Zondervan); *The Anchor Bible* (Doubleday); *The Century Bible* (Thomas Nelson); *New Century Bible* (Butler and Tanner); *Word Bible Commentary* (Word); *Baker Exegetical Commentary on the New Testament* (Baker Books); *The New International Commentary on the New Testament: The Gospel According to John*, rev. ed. (Leon Morris, William B. Eerdmans); and *The Gospel According to John* (D. A. Carson, InterVarsity Press).

5. John Pollard, *Word Bible Commentary* (Dallas: Word Publishing Co., 1993), 371.

6. *The Book of Common Prayer, Collect for the Second Sunday of Advent.*

Chapter 5

1. Walter Brueggemann, *Reverberations of Faith: A Theological Handbook of Old Testament Themes* (Louisville: Westminster John Knox Press, 2002), 118–19.

2. Ibid., 119.

3. Ibid.

4. Christopher J. H. Wright, "Giving the Suffering Their Say," *Christianity Today*, July/August 2015, 87.

5. Annie Dillard, *Pilgrim at Tinker Creek* (New York: Harper's Magazine Press, 1974), 5–6.

6. Romano Guardini, *The Lord* (Washington, DC: Regency Gateway, 1954), 385.

7. Thomas A. Dorsey, "Precious Lord, Take My Hand." Words and music by Thomas A. Dorsey Copyright 1938 (renewed) WARNER TAMERLANE PUBLISHING CORP in the U.S. and UNICHAPPELL MUSIC INC. elsewhere throughout the world. All rights reserved. Lyrics reprinted with permission from Warner Bros. Publications, Miami, FL 33014.

Chapter 6

1. *Luther's Works,* vol. 7, ed. Jaraslov Pelikan (St. Louis: Concordia Press, 1970), 159.

2. John H. Wright, S. J., *A Theology of Christian Prayer* (New York: Pueblo Publishing Co., 1979), 71–72.

3. Bruce Wilkinson, *The Prayer of Jabez: Breaking Through to the Blessed Life* (Colorado Springs: Multnomah Publishers, 2000), 49.

4. Donald G. Bloesch, *The Struggle of Prayer* (San Francisco: Harper and Row, 1980), 71.

5. Wright, *Theology of Christian Prayer,* 74–75.

6. Ibid., 75.

7. Bloesch, *Struggle of Prayer,* 86–89.

8. Swiss theologian Karl Barth said, "To be sure, the God of Holy Scripture is superior to man and the world as the Lord. But he has also bound himself to man and to the world in creating them. God is here introduced to us in the action in which he is engaged, not merely in his superiority over the creature, but also in his relationship to it. What is presented to us is the faithfulness of this God and his living approach to the creature" (Karl Barth, *Church Dogmatics* III.4, *The Doctrine of Creation,* ed. G.W. Bromiley and T.F. Torrence [London: T&T Clark International, 1961], 480).

9. Timothy M. Green, *The God Plot* (Kansas City: Beacon Hill Press of Kansas City, 2014), 59.

10. Karl Barth, *Prayer,* trans. Sarah F. Terrien (Philadelphia: Westminster Press, 1952), 21. Quoted in Bloesch, *Struggle of Prayer,* 74.

11. Brueggemann, *Reverberations of Faith,* 147.

12. Ibid., 148.

13. Bloesch, *Struggle of Prayer,* 72.

14. P. T. Forsyth, *The Soul of Prayer,* 5th ed. (London: Independent Press, 1966), 79. Quoted in Bloesch, *Struggle of Prayer,* 75.

15. Harry Emerson Fosdick, *The Meaning of Prayer* (New York: Association Press, 1916), 63. Quoted in Bloesch, *Struggle of Prayer,* 74.

16. William Law, *The Spirit of Prayer and the Spirit of Love,* ed. Sidney Spencer (Canterbury, England: Clarke, 1969), 120. Quoted in Bloesch, *Struggle of Prayer,* 74.
17. Bloesch, *Struggle of Prayer,* 72–74.
18. Ibid., 74.
19. Elsie Gibson, *Honest Prayer* (Philadelphia: Westminster Press, 1981), 60.
20. Green, *God Plot,* 130.
21. Ibid., 131.
22. Suchocki, *God's Presence,* 18.

Chapter 7

1. Raf Sanchez and Peter Foster, "'You rape our women and are taking over our country,' Charleston church gunman told black victims," *The Telegraph,* June 18, 2015.*http://www.telegraph.co.uk/news/worldnews/northamerica//11684957 You-rape-our-women-and-are-taking-over-our-country-Charleston-church-gunman-told-black-victims.html.* Last accessed 27 January 2016.
2. A county employee made a clerical error when Dylann Roof was arrested on drug charges in February 2015. The error was part of a series of paperwork mix-ups that federal investigators said allowed Roof to buy the gun. "Sheriff Says Clerical Error Enabled Charleston Suspect to Buy Gun," *The Wall Street Journal,* July 14, 2015. *http://www.wsj.com/articles/sheriff-says-clerical-error-enabled-charleston-suspect-to-buy-gun-1436827469.* Last accessed 15 January 2016.
3. Dillard, *Pilgrim at Tinker Creek,* 170.
4. Ibid, 168.
5. Ibid., 131.
6. Ibid., 132.
7. Ibid., 134.
8. Ibid., 28.
9. Ibid., 271.
10. Brueggemann, *Reverberations of Faith,* 213.
11. Ibid.
12. Dillard, *Pilgrim at Tinker Creek,* 265.
13. Ibid., 176.
14. Allies Against Slavery, Austin, Texas, *http://www.alliesagainstslavery.org/slavery/.* Last accessed 18 January 2016.
15. Preston Mendenhall, "Infiltrating Europe's Shameful Trade in Human Beings," nbcnews.com, 2013, *http://www.nbcnews.com/id/3071965/ns/us_news-only/t/infiltrating-europes-shameful-trade-human-beings/#.VaxIh_lVikp.* Last accessed 18 January 2016.
16. Emily Dugan, "The Unstoppable March of the Tobacco Giants," *The Independent,* May 28, 2011. *http://www.independent.co.uk/life-style/health-and-families/health-news/the-unstoppable-march-of-the-tobacco-giants-2290583.html.* Last accessed 18 January 2016.

17. Judith Mackay and John Crofton, "Tobacco and the Developing World," Asian Consultancy on Tobacco Control, Kowloon, Hong Kong; University of Edinburgh, Edinburgh, UK. *http://bmb.oxfordjournals.org/content/52/1/206.full.pdf.* Last accessed 18 January 2016.

18. Dillard, *Pilgrim at Tinker Creek,* 31.

19. Ibid., 33.

20. Hendrik Berkhof, *Christ and the Powers,* trans. John H. Yoder (Scottdale, PA: Herald Press, 1977), 44.

21. Barth, *Church Dogmatics,* IV.3.1, The Doctrine of Reconciliation, 268.

22. Ibid., 196.

23. Ibid.

24. Dillard, *Pilgrim at Tinker Creek,* 268.

Chapter 8

1. C. S. Lewis, *The Screwtape Letters* (New York: New American Library, 1988), 16.

2. Lakewood Church, Houston, Texas, where Joel Osteen is the lead pastor.

3. Joel Osteen, *Every Day a Friday: How to Be Happier 7 Days a Week* (Nashville: FaithWords, 2011).

4. Henri Nouwen, *The Return of the Prodigal Son: A Story of Homecoming* (New York: Doubleday, 1994), 117–18.

Chapter 9

1. "The Chalcedon Formula," Anglicans Online, *http://anglicansonline.org/basics/chalcedon.html.* Last accessed 19 January 2016.

2. John Wesley, "On Discoveries of Faith," Sermon 110, Wesley Center Online, *http://wesley.nnu.edu/john-wesley/the-sermons-of-john-wesley-1872-edition/sermon-110-on-discoveries-of-faith/.* Last accessed 20 January 2016.

Chapter 10

1. Mother Teresa, *Come Be My Light: The Private Writings of the Saint of Calcutta,* ed. Brian Kolodiejchuk (New York: Image, 2009), 20.

Chapter 11

1. Nouwen, *Return of the Prodigal Son,* 129.

Chapter 12

1. Leo Tolstoy, *The Death of Ivan Ilyich* trans. Louise and Aylmer Maude. *http://www.online-literature.com/tolstoy/death-of-ivan-ilych/.* Last accessed 21 January 2016.

2. Ibid.

3. William G. Bixler, "How the Early Church Viewed Martyrs," *Christian History*, July 1, 1990. *http://www.ctlibrary.com/ch/1990/issue27/2728.html*. Last accessed 21 January 2016.

4. Green, *God Plot*, 66–70.

5. Lewis, *Screwtape Letters*, 154.

6. Megan Burns, Mary Beth Dyer, and Michael Bailit, "Reducing Overuse and Misuse: State Strategies to Improve Quality and Cost of Health Care," Robert Wood Johnson Foundation, January 2014, *http://www.ohsu.edu/xd/research/centers-institutes/evidence-based-policy-center/upload/Bailit__Reducing-Overuse-and-Misuse-State-strategies-to-improve-quality.pdf*. Last accessed 21 January 2016.

7. Romano Guardini, *The Lord* (Washington, DC: Regency Gateway, 1954), 114.

8. The sharp separation between the spirit (soul, what is immaterial) and body (what is material, physical) is called dualism. In various forms it characterized much of the Greco-Roman world into which the gospel came. In sharp contrast to the Bible's teaching that God called his whole creation "very good" (Gen. 1:31; Col. 1:15–16) and that the whole creation is the object of redemption (Rom. 8:18–25; Eph. 1:9–10), dualism perceives humans in terms of an inherently good spirit (soul) that is trapped in and burdened by a mortal body from which it seeks release.

9. *The Phaedo*, 114.e, *Plato: The Collected Dialogues*, ed. Edith Hamilton and Huntington Cairns (Princeton, NJ: Princeton University Press, 1961).

10. Ibid., 114c

11. Ibid., 114c–118.

12. Thankfully, Brenda, our daughter, recovered. She is now a mother to two boys, wife to a clergyman, and a special education teacher.

Chapter 13

1. *Collected Works of Flannery O'Connor*, ed. Sally Fitzgerald (New York: Library of America, dist. by Viking Press, 1988), 1067.

2. Flannery O'Connor, *Wise Blood* (New York: Farrar, Straus, and Giroux, 1962), 55.

3. Ibid., 140.

4. Ibid., 184.

5. Ibid., 188.

6. Barth, *Church Dogmatics*, 480 ff.

Conclusion

1. Thomas A. Dorsey, "Precious Lord, Take My Hand."

www.ingramcontent.com/pod-product-compliance
Lightning Source LLC
LaVergne TN
LVHW051557080426
835510LV00020B/3016